Duncan J. D. Smith

ONLY IN
DUBROVNIK

A Guide to Unique Locations,
Hidden Corners and Unusual Objects

Photographs by
Duncan J. D. Smith
except where stated otherwise

**The
Urban
Explorer**

Entrance to the former Benedictine Convent of St. Mary (Samostan sv. Marije) on Ulica od Kaštela (see no. 3)

Contents

Introduction

"The city seems to rise white from the dazzling sea,
its grey walls and bastions one with the rocks that are their foundation."
A Memory of Ragusa (1929) by Leonard Green

Ragusa; Thesaurum mundi; Pearl of the Adriatic: all monikers for the Croatian city of Dubrovnik. Poet and playwright George Bernard Shaw, who visited in 1929, the same year that Leonard Green's little-known memoir was published, was impressed with Dubrovnik's glorious setting between Mount Srđ and the sea and its cultural treasures. Despite an excess of summer visitors, his 'paradise' city continues to enthral.

The origins of Dubrovnik are sketchy. According to Byzantine Emperor Constantine VII (913–959), it was founded in the seventh century AD by refugees from Epidaurum, a nearby Roman city sacked by Slavic tribes. The barren and waterless islet they chose, however, is now known to have been occupied during the early sixth century by a community of Christian Illyrians, with access to several springs. They christened the place Ragusium from the Illyrian word *Lausa* meaning 'rocky'.

By the seventh century, the settlement was under the protection of the Byzantine Emperor. Initially only the islet was occupied, separated from the mainland by a marshy sea channel. The settlement was protected first by a wooden palisade and then a stone wall inside which a large basilica was erected, a forerunner of today's cathedral.

From the turn of the first millennium, Ragusa fell under the alternating suzerainty of Byzantium, Venice and the Normans. It never surrendered its autonomy though and instead prospered through a series of shifting tribute arrangements and trade agreements. During the 11th century, the sea channel was infilled to become the street called Stradun and a pagan Slavic (Croat) settlement called Dubrava on the mainland was absorbed (the name reflected the oaks that grew there). The fortifications were extended to incorporate both settlements creating the footprint of today's world-famous Old Town (Stari Grad).

In 1358, Hungary expelled Venice from the eastern Adriatic. In return for becoming a Hungarian dependent, Ragusa was free to develop into the capital of a tiny but influential aristocratic maritime republic, which reached its commercial peak during the 15th and 16th centuries. A centre of art, literature, theatre and music, with a concomitant love of liberty, it was dubbed the 'Croatian Athens'.

Ragusa's fortunes eventually waned. In 1667, many of the city's distinctive Gothic–Renaissance buildings were toppled by an earthquake. Then, in 1808, the Republic was abolished and incorporated into the Napoleonic Kingdom of Italy (later the Illyrian Provinces). Following the Congress of Vienna (1815), it was made part of the Kingdom of Dalmatia within the Habsburg Empire, where it stayed until the collapse of Austria–Hungary in 1918. Thereafter, as Dubrovnik, it became part of the new Kingdom of Yugoslavia.

Coerced into a Fascist puppet state during the Second World War, Dubrovnik emerged in 1943 as part of the Socialist Republic of Croatia (itself part of the Socialist Federal Republic of Yugoslavia). This lasted forty eight years until 1991, when, in the face of rising Serb nationalism, Croatia declared independence. It did not come without a fight though and for seven months Serb forces besieged Dubrovnik. Croatian victory saw a battle-scarred Dubrovnik restored and promoted to become one of the Mediterranean's great visitor destinations.

Only in Dubrovnik is for independent cultural travellers wishing to delve beneath the city's skin. This is the Dubrovnik of fearsome forts and half-forgotten palaces, saintly relics and vestiges of war, converted convents and cursed islands. The fifty-five locations described represent the author's odyssey in and around the UNESCO-protected Old Town, which together showcase the city's famous and less well-known sights.

Stradun conveniently divides Old Town into two halves. Southwards are many famous sights, including the Baroque Cathedral, with its treasury of religious relics, and the Gothic-Renaissance Rector's Palace and museum. Less well-known are Old Town's mosque and a shop trading on the fact that the necktie is a Croatian invention.

North of Stradun is a smaller, less frequented area, home to Europe's second oldest working synagogue, a beautiful monastic cloister, and the Sponza Palace containing the Ragusan State Statute (1272).

The suburbs of Dubrovnik hold more treasures for those wishing to escape the crowds. They include the atmospheric Boninovo Cemetery, the Rijeka Dubrovačka drowned river valley, and the Red History Museum in the revitalised former industrial district of Gruž. Farther out are singular sights such as the Trsteno Arboretum, the salt pans at Ston, and the ruined holiday resort of Kupari.

Finally there is Dubrovnik's coastline sprinkled with alluring islands, including the dreamy Elaphites, their crumbling churches and noble palaces hidden in the verdant landscape.

Walking is the best way to get around, with buses and boats for the suburbs, islands and beyond. So whether visiting one of Europe's oldest quarantine hospitals, joining a *Game of Thrones'* tour, or dining in a cosy *konoba*, *Only in Dubrovnik* will encourage readers to set out on their own urban expedition.

Duncan J. D. Smith, Dubrovnik & Vienna

1   Walls, Gates and Forts

Old Town (South of Stradun), a walk around the Dubrovnik City Walls (Dubrovačke gradske zidine) starting at the Pile Gate (Vrata od Pila) (note: it can take over an hour to walk the walls in their entirety, with steps, steep paths and few amenities)

Dubrovnik's City Walls (Dubrovačke gradske zidine) have always been a source of civic pride. Considered among the largest and most complete medieval stone fortifications in Europe, they have never been breached. This fact is testament not only to their strength but also to the diplomatic skills of the Ragusans, who remained a free and prosperous trading republic for four and a half centuries. Since 1979, Old Town and its walls have been on UNESCO's list of World Heritage Sites.

The earliest wall was probably a wooden palisade, erected as early as the 6th-century, when Ragusa was an islet occupied by Christian Illyrians, separated from the mainland by a salt-water creek. A defence against seaward Saracens and landward Slavs, it was reworked in limestone during the 8th-century, and then gradually extended. That Ragusa managed to survive a fifteen-month-long siege by the Saracens in the 9th-century proves how well-constructed these early defences were.

During the 11th-century, the creek was infilled and Ragusa extended to include the pagan Slavic (Croat) settlement of Dubrava on the mainland. Between the 12th- and the 17th-centuries, the wall was rebuilt

This aerial view of Dubrovnik's Old Town shows clearly its formidable circuit of limestone walls

resulting in the fortifications seen today. Stretching for 1.2 miles, it attains a maximum height of eighty-two feet and a width of twenty feet. The best way to appreciate it is to make a full perambulation, which is possible from the two main gates: Pile Gate (Vrata od Pila) in the west and Ploče Gate (Vrata od Ploča) in the east.

This walk begins at the Pile Gate, which consists of a 16th-century Renaissance outer gate and a 15th-century Gothic inner gate. Both are adorned with effigies of the city's patron and protector, Saint Blaise (Sveti Blaž). The steps up to the wall are squeezed between the inner gate and the little Church of St. Saviour (Crkva sv. Spasa). To avoid congestion, visitors walk in an anti-clockwise direction.

Embarking on what is a fairly strenuous, hour-long walk, the visitor will immediately notice that the wall is strengthened at various points by additional fortifications, namely three large corner forts, two stand-alone forts, and sixteen semi-circular or quadrangular projecting bastions. One of these is the imposing Fort Bokar (Tvrđava Bokar), which guards the Pile Gate and Pile Bay (Uvala Pile). Completed in 1570 by Bergamasque architect Antonio Ferramolino (d. 1550) to a design by the Florentine architect Michelozzo Michelozzi (1396–1472), it is complemented by the stand-alone Fort Lovrijenac (Tvrđava Lovrijenac) on the opposite side of the bay (see no. 37).

Beyond Fort Bokar, the wall stretches away eastwards along the sea cliffs, punctuated by a number of bastions named (as most are) for various saints. The area between Fort Bokar and the St. Peter (Sv. Petar) Bastion was the first area to be occupied and fortified back in the 6th-century. A permanent archaeological site nearby contains a ruined state granary and two Benedictine convents that stood in Ragusa's first medieval suburb, Na Andriji, which during the 11th-century lay immediately outside the original fortress *(Kaštel)*.

From the St. Margaret (Sv. Margarita) Bastion, the wall turns towards the Old Port (Stara Luka), the southern side of which is protected by the huge Fort St. John (Tvrdava sv. Ivana). Completed in the 1550s to existing plans by the Republic's municipal engineer, Paskoje Miličević (1440–1516), it is accompanied by a second, as yet unexcavated, archaeological field in the medieval suburb of Pustijerna (see no. 15). The port's north side is watched over by the second stand-alone fort, Fort Revelin (Tvrđava Revelin), completed in the 1530s by another Italian architect, Antonio Ferramolino (d. 1550). It protects the Ploče Gate and the city's eastern land approach, and like the Pile Gate consists of an inner and outer gate with drawbridge.

From here, the landward wall runs away westwards. Afforded extra protection by a moat, it was once armed with 120 cannons. The wall is again punctuated by bastions, as well as a modern gate, the Vrata Buža ('hole in the wall'), opened in 1908. The views looking south down Old Town's narrow streets are hugely photogenic, especially when hung with pulley washing lines *(Tiramola)*. The stone loop-holes from which many are strung were originally used for drying skeins of wool and silk when Ragusa was a textile centre.

At the far end stands the final corner fort, the mighty Fort Minčeta (Trđava Minčeta). Again designed by Michelozzi but completed in 1464 by local mason Juraj Dalmatinac (1410–1473), it marks Old Town's highest point and protected the city from the north (see no. 29). Further bastions then punctuate the short stretch of wall between Fort Minčeta and the Pile Gate, where this walk began.

Rough seas between Fort St. John (Tvrdava sv. Ivana) and the St. Saviour (Sv. Spasitelj) Bastion beyond

One of the bastions between Fort Minčeta and the Pile Gate is the Gornji Ugao (Upper Corner) Tower, designed by Michelozzi as part of his remodelling of the western wall. In 2005, archaeologists revealed a late-15th-century foundry here, which unbeknown to most visitors can be explored from inside the walls at the base of Fort Minčeta. Tours take in the impressive casemates *(kazamati)* of Fort Minčeta, the foundry where objects from bells to musket balls were cast until the great earthquake of 1667, a walk along the outside of the western wall, and a tour of Fort Bokar's radially-placed cannon niches, all without the bustle of the well-trodden walls above.

Other locations nearby: 2, 3, 27, 28

2 Onofrio's Fountains

Old Town (South of Stradun), Onofrio's Great and Small Fountains on Stradun

Ragusa during the Middle Ages was a burgeoning city but one that faced a water crisis. This prompted the Ragusan authorities to build an aqueduct to deliver fresh water from afar to the city's fountains and textile industry. Still visible today, the aqueduct and fountains are testament not only to the progressive thinking of the Ragusan Republic but also the architect who made their plans a reality.

Initially, Ragusa took its water from the few brackish wells on the rocky headland on which it was built, as well as cisterns used to collect rainwater from rooftops. In 1311, for example, a large cistern was built outside the city's original customs' house, later rebuilt as the Sponza Palace (Palača Sponza) (the name 'Sponza' is derived from the Latin *spongia* meaning sponge) (see no. 23). During times of drought, ships even brought barrels of fresh water from a spring farther down the coast in Mlini (see no. 46).

By 1436, however, Ragusa was running ever shorter of water. The Great Council decreed that an aqueduct be built to convey water from the spring-fed Ombla Falls (Izvor Omble) at the head of the Rijeka Dubrovačka to the north-east (the name 'Ombla' is Albanian for 'sweet water') (see no. 43). The architect commissioned to undertake the work was Onofrio della Cava, a talented hydraulic engineer from Naples. Between 1436 and 1442, he constructed a gravity-fed aqueduct that brought water from the spring, which lay at an altitude of 350 feet above sea level, down to the city five miles away. Several cisterns were installed along its course, as were a number of watermills. So valuable a commodity was water at this time that anyone caught tampering with the aqueduct faced having their right arm cut off.

Onofrio then set about building two fine public fountains, one at either end of Stradun, Old Town's main thoroughfare. First was Onofrio's Great Fountain (Velika Onofrijeva česma) on Poljana Paskoja Milicevica, just inside the Pile Gate (Vrata od Pila). Completed in 1440, it takes the form of a sixteen-sided reservoir with a domed cupola (a dragon that originally crowned the cupola was lost during the great earthquake of 1667). Each side is decorated with a carved face *(maskeron)*, with a tap projecting from its mouth through which the water flows. See if you can spot the tiny dog figure *(kučak)* on the top of the fountain, installed it is said to protect the city's libertarian values (and possibly its citizens from plague).

Onofrio's Small Fountain (Mala Onofrijeva česma) stands at the opposite end of Stradun, beneath the Bell Tower (Zvonik). Completed in 1442, it was decorated by the Milanese sculptor Pietro di Martino (d. 1473). It supplied a market on Luža ulica, with an extension pipe running to a private fountain in the atrium of the nearby Rector's Palace (Knežev dvor). Later, water was piped out past the Ploče Gate (Vrata od Ploča) to the Tabor, the marketplace of Ragusa's Balkan caravan trade, as well as the Lazareti Quarantine Infirmaries beyond (see nos. 33, 36). Another fountain once stood alongside the Onofrio's Small Fountain for use exclusively by Ragusa's Jewish community. It was later removed to Brsalje ulica outside the Pile Gate, where it can still be seen.

Detail of the Large Onofrian Fountain (Velika Onofrijeva česma) on Poljana Paskoja Milicevica

Only in the mid-20th-century did Dubrovnik receive a new water system at which point Onofrio's aqueduct was abandoned. Its course, however, can still be traced across the hillside overlooking the city by following the stone slabs used to cover the water channel.

Other locations nearby: 1, 3, 27

3 The Orphan's Window

Old Town (South of Stradun), the former Convent of St. Clare (Samostan Sveta Klare) just inside the Pile Gate (Vrata od Pila) on Poljana Paska Miličevića

Old Town during the heyday of the Ragusan Republic contained over thirty churches, and eight monasteries and convents. The reason for multiple convents was because noble families only provided a dowry for their eldest daughter. Younger ones were placed in convents, where they remained until the age of fourteen, at which point they were prepared for marriage. Three Old Town convents are still standing although they now serve different purposes.

One is the former Convent of St. Clare (Samostan sv. Klare) on Poljana Paska Miličevića. It was founded in 1290 by the Franciscan contemplative Order of Poor Clares. In 1432, Ragusa's progressive Great Council put them in charge of one of the world's first state orphanages. Located around the corner on Zlatarićeva ulica, a part of its façade still stands, comprising a bricked-up doorway and two barred windows. It was through the window on the right, the so-called Orphan's Window that unwanted infants were passed by means of a revolving cylinder of the type used to deliver goods discreetly to closed convents. Although no questions were asked, the Latin inscription over the doorway – *Cochalvit cor meu itra me* (My heart chastises me) – must have left a bitter taste. Once inside, the babies were baptised and cared for until the age of six, when they were offered up for adoption. Young mothers in the process of childbirth were given a piece of what the nuns believed to be Jesus' swaddling clothes for protection (see no. 11).

In 1808, the orphanage was closed by order of Napoleon, as were all Ragusa's religious houses. Thereafter it served as an ammunition storehouse and a stable, and was later largely demolished. Of the convent itself, the cloistered courtyard serves today as a summertime restaurant space.

Two other repurposed convents exist in this part of Old Town. Most atmospheric is the former Benedictine Convent of St. Mary (Samostan sv. Marije) at the corner of Ulica Svete Marije and Ulica od Kaštela (the latter street name is important as it reminds passers-by that the first fort in Ragusa built as early as the 6th-century stood here). The convent was established on the site during the 12th-century, rebuilt three centuries later, and reworked following the devastating earthquake of 1667. The street name also explains the name of the conventual Church of St. Mary of the Castle (Crkva svete Marije od Kaštela), which was built around 1500 by the Andrijić family firm of stonemasons from Korčula, with its Gothic elements and a Renaissance semi-circular apse.

As with the Convent of St. Clare, the convent was dissolved by Napoleon, and then converted into a French barracks. Later the entire complex, church included, was given over to private dwellings, the entrance to which can be found at the top of Ulica Svete Marije (note the tympanum depicting the Angel Gabriel appearing to Mary over which hang the coats of arms of Dubrovnik and the noble families who endowed the convent).

The third convent is the former Dominican Convent of St. Katherine of Siena (Samostan sv. Katarine Sijenske) *on the corner of Ulica Josipa Jurja Strossmayera and Crijevićeva ulica*. Built over an early medieval Church of St. Peter the Great (Crkva sv. Petra Velikog), which was destroyed during the great earthquake of 1667, its Baroque church now serves as the concert hall of the Luka Sorkočević Art School (Umjetnička Škola Sorkočevića), named for the renowned 18th-century Ragusan composer (see no. 17). Again note the street entrance tympanum depicting various saints.

Unwanted infants were once passed through this window on Zlatarićeva ulica

Other locations nearby: 1, 2, 5

4   A Granary Repurposed

Old Town (South of Stradun), the Rupe Ethnographic Museum (Ethnografic Museum Rupe) at Ulica Od Rupa 3

Dubrovnik has a good track record when it comes to adapting old buildings to new uses. They include a night club inside a 500-year-old fortress, a brewery in an early-20th-century salt warehouse, and a museum in Socialist-era factory (see nos. 31, 41, 42). Most extraordinary of all is the Rupe Ethnographic Museum (Ethnografic Museum Rupe), which occupies an impressive late-16th-century granary.

The museum's popular name of 'Rupe' translates as 'holes'. This curious nickname, as well as the name of the street on which the museum stands, refers to the granary completed in 1590 to plans by a builder from Apulia. It consists of fifteen great bottle-shaped pits cut into the bedrock, each with a capacity of just over 500 tons. In these 'holes' the Ragusan Republic stored its reserves of wheat, barley and millet, imported from as far away as Albania and the Crimea. A lining of hydraulic cement kept the grains at a constant temperature of 17°C to prevent them from spoiling. The reserves could keep the city supplied for up to six months in case of a prolonged siege, and so important were they that Ulica Siroka, the road leading up to the granary, was permitted to be made broader than other side roads by a specific clause in the Ragusan State Statute.

Originally a four-storey building stood over the pits, in which the grain was dried prior to being dropped through chutes into the pits below. During the great earthquake of 1667, however, this was badly damaged and subsequently rebuilt as the three-storey structure seen today. It is the last surviving example of several state granaries that once existed in Old Town, including one beneath the Rector's Palace (Knežev dvor).

As for the Ethnographic Museum, its holdings were first assembled from a variety of sources during the first decades of the 20th-century. These included private donations, notably 2,500 items from Jelka Miš (1875–1956), a local teacher with a passion for folk art and traditional costume. Starting out in 1895 from the Konavle district, south-east of Dubrovnik, she travelled widely, documenting regional embroidery and dyeing techniques, and preserving fabric samples that otherwise would have been lost to history. Her own handiwork gained considerable renown, with a handmade tablecloth finding its way into the hands of American President Woodrow Wilson.

When it first opened to the public in 1950, the Ethnographic Museum was housed in Old Town's Fort St. John (Tvrdava sv. Ivana). Later, in 1991, it relocated to the old granary, where today it contains some 6,500 artefacts reflecting the traditional heritage of Croatia.

On the first floor, the museum documents rural architectural styles, peasant husbandry and traditional festivities. Old agricultural implements and some fascinating photographs of such tools still in use are used to illustrate skills such as basket weaving, fish trap manufacture and beekeeping

The second floor is home to an important collection of folk costume and textile handiwork displays from Dubrovnik and the adjacent coastal regions (Rijeka Dubrovačka to the north and Župa Dubrovačka to the south), as well as Konavle, the Pelješac Peninsula, and the islands, including the Elaphites, Mljet, Lastovo and distant Korčula. Rarities include samples of Dubrovnik lace, known as *Point de Raguse*, which today has almost disappeared, and Konavle silk embroidery applied to women's bodices and cuffs, with its bold geometric motifs in red and green on a brown-black base (see back cover). The display of corn dollies in a separate cabinet is a nice albeit tenuous reminder of the original purpose of the museum building.

Other locations nearby: 3, 5

5 Who was Marin Držić?

Old Town (South of Stradun), the House of Marin Držić (Marin Držićs hus) at Ulica Široka 7

Outside the Gradska Kavarna café at Ulica Pred Dvorom 1 (Old Town) there is a bronze statue by Croatian sculptor Ivan Meštrović (1883–1962). It depicts a monkish-looking scribe, his Roman nose buffed to a shine for luck by passers-by. According to an inscription on the pedestal, this is Marin Držić (1508–1567), Croatia's finest Renaissance comic playwright. Revered in his homeland, most outsiders will probably ask who he was.

Držić was born in 1508, one of a dozen children of merchant parents fallen on hard times. Despite his rebel temperament, in 1526 he entered the priesthood and was sent to Siena to study Church Canon Law. Although his academic achievements were modest, his outgoing personality endeared him to his professors, who elected him a university rector. He eventually lost interest though and in 1543 returned to Ragusa.

Back home Držić became acquainted with an Austrian adventurer, one Count Rogendorf. Rogendorf spent time in Constantinople, where he may have been a double-agent serving both the Austrians and the Ottomans. Držić made use of his exposure to this colourful world of intrigue when a few years later he commenced his literary career.

Držić's writing spanned several genres: lyric poetry, pastorals, political letters and pamphlets. It is his comedies, however, which are best remembered and now considered among the finest in European Renaissance literature. As with later comedy writers like Lope de Vega, Ben Jonson and Molière, they are full of life, celebrating liberty and truth whilst also exposing greed and egotism, in both family and the state.

Držić's first play *Pomet* was premiered in 1548 but is now lost. He followed this with the largely intact *Dundo Maroje*, which was first staged in 1551 at the Rector's Palace *(Knežev dvor)*. Like all classical comedy, it is a moralising work built around a zig-zagging plot. The play's eponymous hero is a Dubrovnik merchant, who dispatches his son Maro to Rome with 5,000 ducats to conduct a business deal. Along the way Maro squanders the money on wine and women prompting his father to follow him for a showdown. Maro is initially hostile towards his father, who attempts to restore his son's loyalty. Meanwhile, observing from behind the scenes is Pomet, a canny manservant based on Držić himself, who reminds the reader that there is no real difference between good and bad people, and that society should be equal. Although the ending of the play is not preserved, enough remains to identify it as one of the most enduring works of Croatian drama.

Držić is credited with bringing modern theatrical techniques of plotting and suspense to what were hitherto rather simplistic comedies, in much the same way that William Shakespeare later did in England. Similarly he used everyday parlance to bring authenticity to his characters and to make them accessible to the audience. In so doing, Držić made Croatian drama not only a form of entertainment but also a satire on the times.

A well-known critic of the Ragusan Republic,

The statue of playwright *Marin Držić* on Ulica Pred Dvorom

which was essentially an oligarchy run by a group of aristocratic families, Držić spent his last years in Venice. There he wrote letters to the powerful Medici family, requesting their help in overthrowing the Republic and restoring power to the people. They did not respond.

Although Držić died in poverty, his works are a reminder that Ragusa during the 16th-century acted as an incubator for literature and theatre. To get closer to Držić and his *œuvre*, one should visit his former home at Ulica Široka 7 (Old Town), where there is an exhibition illustrating his life and work.

Other locations nearby: 3, 7, 8

6   What a Big Street!

Old Town (South of Stradun), Stradun street between Pile Gate (Vrata od Pila) and the Old Port (Stara Luka)

Dubrovnik's Old Town (Stari Grad) is divided into two unequal parts by Stradun, the city's main arterial thoroughfare. It runs for almost a fifth of a mile from the Pile Gate (Vrata od Pila) in the west to the Old Port (Stara Luka) in the east. Locals sometimes call it Placa, a word derived from the Latin *platea*, which simply means 'street'. The name Stradun, however, has a more colourful origin. It was allegedly coined by an Italian officer in the Austrian army, who upon seeing the street for the first time declared "Che stradone!" (What a big street!). It seems more likely though that the name dates back to the Middle Ages, when the street was first laid out and made the rest of Ragusa's streets appear narrow by comparison.

During the sixth-century, when Christian Illyrian settlers first arrived in what is now Old Town, the site was little more than a rocky islet, separated from the wooded mainland by a salt-water creek. They set about building the first iteration of Ragusa. Later, during the 11th-century, the creek was infilled and the pagan Slavic (Croat) settlement of Dubrava on the other side absorbed. With the town's circuit wall extended to incorporate both settlements, the infilled channel became the first incarnation of what by the 13th-century would be Ragusa's main street.

Stradun was initially surfaced with red bricks, which were replaced in the mid-15th-century with flagstones. The glassy limestone paving seen today dates from 1901. Similarly, the buildings that line Stradun have changed over the years. It is not clear exactly what the first structures looked like but by the 17th-century the Gothic-Renaissance palaces of the well-to-do stood here. All were toppled by the great earthquake of 1667, with the exception of the Sponza Palace (Palača Sponza) at the east end (see no. 23). Other survivals included the two 15th-century Onofrio Fountains at either end of Stradun, and the little Renaissance-style Church of St. Saviour (Crkva sv. Spasa), just inside the Pile Gate (see no. 2). Built by the Andrijić family firm of stonemasons, it commemorated the victims of an earlier earthquake in 1520.

After the earthquake, Stradun was remodelled by Roman papal architect, Giulio Cerruti. Recent studies suggest he based his designs on those of pre-earthquake communal houses designed by French architect Jacques de Spinis. Unlike the previous palaces, the new builds were restrained, all of a uniform height, and with the same configuration of rooms. This consisted of retail premises at street level with an arched doorway and display window, and a store room to the rear; a first and second storey reserved for residential use; and a loft kitchen so positioned to prevent the spread of fire, as had occurred during the earthquake.

Stradun still looks much the same today, with its buildings book-ended by bell towers *(zvonici)*, one attached to the Franciscan Monastery (Franjevaäki samostan) at the west end, the other built in 1444 at the opposite end, with its bell struck every half hour by two verdigreed bronze soldiers known locally as the Green Men (see no. 27). Inevitably Stradun has long been a popular promenade

Stradun looking west towards the Franciscan Monastery (Franjevaäki samostan)

including the annual Feast of Saint Blaise (Sveti Blaž) procession each 3rd February, as well as New Year's Eve celebrations and occasional concerts.

Whilst walking along Stradun one should occasionally glance downwards. The surface of the paving slabs is pockmarked here and there with starburst shrapnel marks from the Croatian War of the early 1990s (see nos. 26, 40).

Other locations nearby: 7, 25, 26

7 An Orthodox Place of Worship

Old Town (South of Stradun), the Serbian Orthodox Church of the Holy Annunciation (Srpske pravoslavne crkve Svetog blagoveštenja) at Ulica od Puča 8

Whether they are Orthodox Christians, Jews or Muslims, the story of Dubrovnik's religious minorities is a fascinating one (see nos. 8, 25). During the time of the Ragusan Republic, people of various faiths were drawn by the city's growing prosperity. Citizenship, however, was difficult to attain since Roman Catholicism was the state religion and applications could only be ratified by Ragusan officials with a majority vote. Non-Catholic denominations were kept from building their own places of worship inside the city walls until well after the Republic's fall in 1808.

The quest to establish Dubrovnik's Orthodox community began during the second half of the 18th-century. At this time the Republic enjoyed protective tributary status under the Ottomans albeit with Russian interference to maintain a foothold in the Balkans. Russia went so far as to formally request that Ragusa accept a Russian consul, one with the right to erect an Orthodox church. The consul arrived but the church was rejected on the grounds that Ragusa was home to too few Orthodox families (the real fear for Ragusa though was the prospect of a destabilising influx of Orthodox Christians from regions under Ottoman control, notably Bosnia and Herzegovina). Instead the Russian consul was initially allowed a private chapel in his residence followed later by a public chapel in the district of Boninovo, well outside the city walls. The chapel's priest could visit Ragusa but only twice a year and even then only for a maximum of eight days.

Not until 1813 were Ragusa's Orthodox Christians permitted to gain citizenship more easily. In 1837, as their number increased, they opened a dedicated cemetery at Boninovo, all the while maintaining their religious affiliation with the Serbian Orthodox Church (see no. 39). Eventually, in 1848, Orthodoxy was granted equal status with Catholicism by which time there were several hundred Orthodox immigrants in the city. One of them was the popular Serbian author Milovan Glišić (1847–1908), who died in Dubrovnik and was buried in the cemetery.

Next began the task of securing a site within the Old Town walls on which to build an Orthodox church. In 1868, with financial assistance from wealthy merchant Božo Bošković (1815–1879), land was acquired from Frano Getaldić-Gundulić (1833–1899), a proponent of the Serb-Catholic Movement in Dubrovnik, on Ulica od Puča. Work on the church started in 1871 and construction was largely completed by 1877. The result as seen by visitors today is a single nave structure, with a semicircular apse and a pair of octagonal belfries. As befits the Orthodox liturgy, the style is neo-Byzantine and as such stands out from Old Town's many Roman Catholic edifices. Inside, the church preserves its original coffered ceiling, with a magnificent iconostasis made in Greece. Above it is a frieze depicting the Last Supper, flanked by the Baptism of Christ (left) and the Annunciation (right).

In 1907, the neighbouring Bundic Palace was acquired to house a collection of Greek, Italian, Russian and Slovenian icons. Currently closed for renovation, it contains examples from as early as the 15th-century, as well as more recent works painted by the Cavtat-born artist Vlaho Bukovac (1855–1922). There is also a copy of the Miroslav Gospels (1897), a collection of priests' robes and altar vessels, and portraits of famous Ragusans. The church owns an extensive library, too, which includes works written in Church Slavonic (the Slavic liturgical language used by the Orthodox Church in the Balkans) and an Orthodox service book *(Menologium)* printed in Kiev in 1703.

A gilded icon in the Serbian Orthodox Church of the Holy Annunciation (Srpske pravoslavne crkve Svetog blagoveštenja)

Other locations nearby: 5, 6, 8, 26

8 A Dubrovnik Mosque

Old Town (South of Stradun), the Dubrovnik Mosque (Masjid Dubrovnik) at Ulica Miha Pracata 3 (note: visitors to the mosque's prayer hall must remove their shoes and leave them in the rack outside)

Muslims have passed through Dubrovnik for centuries. Originally they came as merchants, officials of the Ottoman Empire, and pilgrims since Dubrovnik lay on the European leg of the pilgrimage route to Mecca. However, it was only after the abolition of the Ragusan Republic in 1808 that the first Muslims actually settled in the city.

A key date in the story of Dubrovnik's Muslims is 1878. In this year under the terms of the Congress of Berlin, Bosnia and Herzegovina were integrated into the Austro-Hungarian Empire. Unlike Dubrovnik, Muslims had been settled in Bosnia and Herzegovina since the area was conquered by the Ottomans in the 15th-century. With Dalmatia and Herzegovina now geographical neighbours, the first Muslim families freely crossed the old border to settle permanently in Dubrovnik.

The early years of the 20th-century saw the commercial development of Dubrovnik's port of Gruž. This attracted labourers and merchants alike, some of whom were again Muslims drawn in from Herzegovina. By the 1920s, Dubrovnik's still modest Muslim community began organising itself in terms of a place to worship, with prayers initially held in private homes. It is known, for example, that in 1929 worship took place in the house of the Karamehmedovic family. As the community grew, however, this inevitably cramped arrangement became inadequate and by the early 1930s the search was on for more suitable premises.

On 24th July 1933, Dubrovnik's Muslims formed themselves into an official Islamic community or *Majlis*, and appointed an Imam to lead their congregational worship. Two years later, in 1935, they were granted a dedicated space for burials at the Boninovo Cemetery (Groblje Boninovo) complete with facilities for the ritual washing and shrouding of the deceased *(ghusl)* (see no. 39). Still the search continued for a permanent play in which to pray. In 1937, for example, a sympathetic goldsmith by the name of Josip Krilic leased the community a storeroom on Ulica Dinka Ranjine in Old Town. A lack of water, however, which is necessary for Islamic ablutions, saw the community soon move on to a temporary third floor space behind the nearby Church of St. Blaise (Crkva sv. Blaža). Still the search continued until

The stepped pulpit (minbar) of the Dubrovnik Mosque (Masjid Dubrovnik) on Ulica Miha Pracata

1941, when the community finally leased a former noble's house at Ulica Miha Pracata 3. This they purchased in 1964 and the community, which currently numbers around 3,000 individuals, has been happily worshipping there ever since.

The three-storey building is well worth visiting for those with an interest in Islam. The all-important prayer hall *(Masjid)* can be found on the first floor (visitors must leave their shoes in the shoe racks outside). It features arched wooden windows, a large carpet on which guidelines are marked to show where male worshippers should kneel, and a stepped pulpit *(minbar)* from where the imam delivers his sermons. That the top of the *minbar* extends into a space in the ceiling is a reminder that the roof of the building was damaged in the early 1990s during the Croatian War and later rebuilt at a lower level.

The mosque also features a religious instruction room *(Mektebi)*, a library, offices and a youth club. In common with most mosques, prayers are said at noon *(dhur)*, dusk *(magreb)* and at night *('isha)*, with the main prayer day being Friday.

Other locations nearby: 7, 9, 10

9 Hotels with History

Old Town (South of Stradun), a handful of historic hotels, including the Pucić Palace at Od Puča 1

Visitors to Dubrovnik will find all manner of accommodation from rooms-to-let to grand hotels and former palaces. Inevitably the latter come with a bigger price tag but also a greater chunk of history. What follows is a handful of the best.

Located in the centre of Old Town, the Pucić Palace at Ulica Od Puča 1 began life in the 17th-century as a family home. It was built by the influential Pucić family (known also as Pozze or Poce), their aristocratic roots stretching back a further four centuries. Politicians, clerics, writers and artists, their number included Karlo Pavlov Poce, who in the 15th-century published Dubrovnik's first poetry book. Patrons of the arts, they supported Cavtat-born Vlaho Bukovac (1855–1922), one of Croatia's greatest modern painters. As with many of the city's Gothic–Renaissance buildings, the Pucić Palace was damaged by the great earthquake of 1667. The arched alleyway on Ulica Dinka Ranjine down one side of the building marks where the original building was rent in two. Whilst half the building remained intact, its neighbours were toppled, their place taken later by Gundulićeva poljana, today Old Town's marketplace (see no. 10). In 1895, the palace received a new owner, who converted it into a hotel. Damaged during the Croatian War of the early 1990s, it was restored according to UNESCO guidelines so as to showcase its original structural merits. Reopened in 2002, the 5-star hotel today offers history and modernity in abundance, including original vaulted marble staircases, and new hand-woven carpets on olive wood floors.

Also in Old Town but a little less grand is the Hotel Stari Grad at Ulica Od Sigurate 4. Its aristocratic origins are similar to those of the Pucić Palace in that it was originally a nobleman's house, albeit one built a century earlier. The old stone façade belies the contemporary decoration of its eight bedrooms.

For glamour, one should look outside Old Town. On the sea cliffs to the south, along Ulica Frana Supila and Ulica Vlaha Bukovca, stand half a dozen upscale hotels with stories to tell. First is the Excelsior, which comprises the former private Villa Odak (1913), a modern wing called the Tower, and the red-roofed Villa Agave on the rocks below. Sitting over the remains of a 16th-century Chapel of St. Lazarus, which served the nearby quarantine hospital, the latter was occupied in the

A statue of poet Ivan Gundulić looks over to the Pucić Palace hotel

1870s as the Casa San Lazzaro by Arthur Evans (1851–1941), a British newspaper journalist who later found fame as a Cretan archaeologist (see no. 33).

Next is the Grand Villa Argentina, which again comprises several parts: the Grand Villa proper built in 1922, where Richard Burton and Elizabeth Taylor, Maria Callas, and Herbert von Karajan were hosted; the Villa Orsula, formerly a private villa built in 1936; and the elite turquoise-domed Villa Sheherezade (Vila Šeherezada), completed in 1929 as a private home for Estonian businessman William Zimdin (1880–1951).

Finally, there is the Villa Dubrovnik built in 1961 to a Modernist concrete design by Zagreb-trained architect Mladen Frka. Originally a residence for the country's political elite, it became a hotel in 1963.

West of Old Town stands the imposing Hilton Imperial, Dubrovnik's first purpose-built hotel, opened in 1895 to promote the health benefits of sea bathing. Farther west, on the Lapad Peninsula, there is the Hotel Lapad, a family-owned palace once known as the White Castle, and the Kazbek, which occupies the former 16th-century summer villa of the noble Zamanja family.

Other locations nearby: 8, 10, 11, 20, 21, 22

10 Markets Old and New

Old Town (South of Stradun), the Morning Market on Gundulićeva poljana

Dubrovnik has two open-air markets and both are worth experiencing. The Morning Market is held most days on Gundulićeva poljana, Old Town's largest square. It is overlooked by the periwigged statue of Ragusa's two-time rector and great Renaissance poet, Ivan Gundulić (1589–1638) (see nos. 5, 18). In days gone by the emphasis here was on basic foodstuffs and household items. These days the product range is inevitably aimed at visitors, too. As well as home-grown fruit and vegetables, there are stalls selling locally-made lace and embroidery, pouches of dried lavender, dried and candied fruits, locally-produced olive oil and honey. There are also bottles of sweet fruit liqueurs *(Slatki Likeri)* made from rose petals (ruža), carob (rogač), myrtle (mirta) and mandarin (mandarina). Other locally-produced drinks include grape *loza* and herbal *travarica*, both of which are particular to the Croatian coast. Saturday is the busiest day, when the stallholders remain until late afternoon (during the week some pack up from as early as noon).

Gruž Market at Obala Stjepana Radića 21, north-west of Old Town, is a morning-only affair and can easily be reached by bus. The location here is also historic insomuch as the market takes place in the former garden of the noble Gundulić family's villa, one of several wealthy summer retreats that occupied the once-separate town of Gruž before it became Dubrovnik's industrialised zone during the 19th-century (see nos. 41, 42). The clientele consists predominantly of locals and restaurateurs, so there is a broader array of foodstuffs than in Old Town and the prices are more reasonable.

Producers come from far and wide to sell their goods at Gruž. Fruit and vegetable growers come from Primorje in the fertile Neretva basin, on Fridays fish and shellfish are brought over from the Elaphiti Islands (Elafitski otoci), while other traders come from Konavle and Župa Dubrovačka, south-east of Dubrovnik, and Herzegovina over the border.

It is worth remembering that Gruž Market is popular with commercial buyers so business starts and finishes early (7am–12pm) and the stock varies from day to day depending on seasonal availability. Fridays are the best days to attend according to those in the know. They include vegetarian triathlete Ivo Dadić, who sources many of the ingredients here for the plant-based menu served in his popular restaurant

Urban & Veggie at nearby Obala Stjepana Radića 13.

The Dubrovnik region boasts olive groves, vineyards and orchards producing superb lemons, oranges, carobs, pomegranates, figs, and quince used in curd tartlets *(Kontonjata)*. The many hours of sunshine and low rainfall guarantees good seasonal crops of salad and root vegetables, aubergines, artichokes, courgettes and chard, as well as a wide array of culinary herbs. Potential purchases at both markets might include cabbage for preparing *zelena menestra* (a traditional smoked pork, cabbage and potato stew), goat's cheese for salads, eggs for *rožata* (Croatian-style crème caramel), and oranges from the island of Lopud for orange sponge cake.

Xenia Capor sells her ceramic fruits at Old Town's longstanding Morning Market

The reputation of the writer Ivan Gundulić, whose statue watches over Old Town's Morning Market, rests on three great works: the pastoral play *Dubravka* (premiered in Ragusa in 1628), with its powerful celebration of liberty; the religious poem *Suze sina razmetnoga* (Tears of the Prodigal Son) (1622), in which he presents the three categories of Christianity; and the epic poem *Osman* (1652), an assertion of Croatian national identity under Ottoman suzerainty (his statue, erected during the 19th-century, evoked a similar sense of national consciousness during Austrian rule). Gundulić was an advocate of the south Slavic Shtokavian dialect, which underpins the modern Croatian language.

Other locations nearby: 8, 11, 12, 18, 20, 21

11   Cathedral Curiosities

**Old Town (South of Stradun), the Cathedral of the Assumption
(Katedrala Velike Gospe) at Ulica kneza Damjana Jude 1**

According to legend, in 1192 the English King Richard the Lionheart (1157–1199) was shipwrecked on the Croatian island of Lokrum. Returning home from the Third Crusade, it is said he offered to build a votive chapel on the island in return for shelter (see no. 55). When the Ragusans received him with great ceremony he instead offered to build them a cathedral within their city walls. In actual fact, however, the cathedral known officially as the Cathedral of the Assumption (Katedrala Velike Gospe) was built well before Richard set out on his crusade, and was financed by gifts from the Ragusan nobility.

Archaeological excavations have demonstrated the existence of two earlier structures on the cathedral's site at Ulica kneza Damjana Jude 1 (Old Town): a 7th-century Byzantine basilica and a splendid 12th-century Romanesque cathedral (see nos. 14, 17). The latter was toppled by the great earthquake of 1667 but not before the Archbishop of Dubrovnik, Giovanni Angelo Medici (1499–1565) of Milan, became Pope Pius IV, a sign of the the city's prestige. After the earthquake, the Ragusan Senate commissioned Italian architect Andrea Buffalini to draft plans for a new cathedral, the one seen today. Baroque in style, with a cruciform plan and cupola, it was completed in 1713 by various Italian and Ragusan stonemasons. Over the main altar hangs Titian's polyptych of the *Assumption of the Virgin Mary* (1552).

Impressive as the architecture of the cathedral is, the Cathedral Treasury (Riznica Katedrale) is what many visitors will remember. Here reside more than 130 relics of saints and martyrs dating from between the 11th- and 20th-centuries. They are contained in gold and silver reliquaries, often in the shape of the saint's body part, and mostly crafted by Ragusan metalworkers.

Chief among the relics are those of the city's patron, Saint Blaise (Sveti Blaž), which are paraded through the streets on the saint's feast day (February 3rd) (see no. 21). The Reliquary of the Head of Saint Blaise takes the form of a Byzantine crown decorated with medallions of saints and enamel ornaments, and probably dates to the 11th-century. The Reliquary of the Right Hand was created a century later and features a large blue stone surrounded by pearls. The Reliquary of the Foot was made by Byzantine goldsmiths in the 11th-century and is covered in filigree. All three relics are displayed in a cabinet at the front

Reliquary of the Hand of Saint Blaise in the Cathedral of the Assumption (Katedrala Velike Gospe)

of the treasury alongside a 16th-century glass-sided silver chest contains nothing less than Jesus' swaddling clothes. The Reliquary of the Throat of Saint Blaise, however, which takes the form of a 15th-century silver monstrance with a crystal window, stands separately to the left of the main treasury Crucifix and is invoked by those with throat conditions. The Crucifix itself holds a piece of wood from the Holy Cross, as do the two reliquaries above it.

The treasury also contains a gold-plated dish and jug decorated with lizards and Mediterranean plants made for the Hungarian King Matthias Corvinus, an *Adoration of the Magi* triptych used by Ragusan envoys *(poklisari)* as a travelling altarpiece during their visits to the Ottoman sultan, and a copy of Raphael's *Madonna della Seggiola* said to be by the master's hand.

In 1979, the cathedral was struck again by an earthquake only this time most of the damage could be repaired. This was also the case in 1991 when it was hit by a missile during the Croatian War.

Other locations nearby: 9, 10, 12, 13, 16, 20

12 A Different Natural History Museum

Old Town (South of Stradun), the Dubrovnik Natural History Museum (Prirodoslovni muzej Dubrovnik) at Ulica Androvićeva 1

A visit to a natural history museum might not be high on the 'to do' list of some visitors to Dubrovnik. The Dubrovnik Natural History Museum (Prirodoslovni muzej Dubrovnik), however, is a little different. Yes, there are stuffed creatures here but it's the way they are displayed that is novel, with many liberated from the confines of their traditional cabinets to inhabit striking wall-mounted displays against some unexpected backdrops. This ensures that visitors of all ages are kept both informed and engaged.

The museum at Ulica Androvićeva 1 (Old Town) has its origins in the Museo Patrio (Patriotic Museum), Dubrovnik's first museum institution. Initially a repository for artefacts of local and regional interest, it was financed by Dubrovnik's Chamber of Commerce and Industry, which saw it as beneficial not only for Dubrovnik but also for the education of its children.

The Chamber's president, the wealthy pharmacist and ship-owner Antun Drobac (1810–1882), got things started by donating his own private natural history collection, which included a large collection of molluscs. He then launched a campaign to collect all manner of specimens not only from Croatia but also well beyond the borders of the Austro-Hungarian Empire, which governed Dubrovnik at the time. The response was strong, including Nile and Red Sea invertebrates from a local priest, minerals from a Croatian in California, a crate of stones from St. Petersburg, and a collection of algae courtesy of Marija Selebam de Cattani (1789–1870), Croatia's first female botanist. In 1873, with so many artefacts now to hand, it was decided to open the museum to the public.

After Drobac's death, the museum's holdings were bolstered with further specimens, notably fish collected locally by naturalist Baldo Kosić (1829–1918). Neither man, however, would recognise the museum today. Since their time, it has changed address no less than five times, and many specimens have been lost to war, earthquake and under-funding. What remained was carefully gathered together at the current address, a restored 16th–17th-century palace, in 2009.

The long story of the museum's physical journey is detailed throughout the three-storey building, alongside examples of traditional taxidermy. The greater part of the museum, however, has been given a more contemporary feel in tune with the demands of a modern and often young audience. Thus, a huge Adriatic Leatherback Turtle *(Dermochelys coriacea)* swims lazily across the floor in one room, a collection of desiccated sea creatures dangle among discarded compact discs in another, and elsewhere there is a series of wall paintings of pop singer Freddy Mercury strutting his stuff as a fish! A great strength of

Dubravka Tullio's fishy Freddy Mercury at the Museum of Natural History (Prirodoslovni muzej Dubrovnik)

the museum is its didactic approach, including creative workshops, laboratory and field visits, and special events to mark International Museum Day and Nature Protection Day.

As a pharmacist Antun Drobac invented Pyrethrum Powder, a natural insecticide derived from the Tansy Daisy *(Tanacetum cinerarii folium)*. The discovery helped contain the cholera epidemic that hit Dubrovnik in 1867 and it is still used today. As a shipowner, he furnished his vessels with pharmacies, one of which is preserved in Dubrovnik's Maritime Museum (see no. 15). Remarkably, these weren't Drobac's only achievements. A freelance daguerreotypist, he has been hailed as the country's first photographer, and in 1847 he administered ether for the first time in Croatia. Little wonder Dubrovnik has a street named after him and a bronze bust by Croatian sculptor Ivan Rendić (1849–1932) stands in the museum courtyard. A reconstruction of Drobac's study can be found in the Rector's Palace (Knežev dvor) (see no. 18).

Other locations nearby: 10, 11, 13, 14, 16

13 The Jesuit Steps

Old Town (South of Stradun), the Jesuit Steps (Skale od Jezuita) on Ulica uz Jezuite and the Church of St. Ignatius (Crkva sv. Ignacija) on Poljana Ruđera Boškovića (note: English-language Mass is celebrated at 11am on Sundays between June and September)

Everyone knows the Spanish Steps in Rome but what about the Jesuit Steps (Skale od Jezuita) in Dubrovnik? While they may not have hosted Audrey Hepburn and Cary Grant in the film *Roman Holiday*, they are still a magnet for visitors and no less crowded. Together with the Jesuit church and college at their summit, they form a unique Baroque ensemble.

The Jesuits, known formally as the Society of Jesus, were founded in 1540 by Spanish priest and theologian, Ignatius of Loyola (1491–1556). With their vow of obedience to the Pope and zeal for teaching and missionary work, they arrived in Ragusa during the mid-16th-century. The Renaissance style was in vogue at the time but within a century it had given way to Baroque. A comparatively flamboyant Italianate style, it was embraced by the Jesuits across Europe as a means of asserting the Catholic Counter-Reformation.

Prior to the steps being constructed, a simple dirt track connected Gundulićeva Poljana, the square down by the Cathedral, with Poljana Ruđera Boškovića above. Here following the great earthquake of 1667, the Jesuits built their Baroque Church of St. Ignatius (Crkva sv. Ignacija). Designed by Italian Jesuit brother and architect Andrea Pozzo (1642–1709), it was modelled like many Jesuit churches of the period on the Church of the Gesù in Rome, the Society's mother church (the first of Pozzo's commissions outside Rome, he later designed the Jesuit Church in Vienna and Cathedral in Ljubljana).

Completed in 1725, the church is impressive from most vantage points, its massive buttressed flanks rising high above the surrounding rooftops, and even the nearby city wall, from where a huge *IHS*, the Jesuits' vowel-free form of the name Jesus, can be seen. The impressive church doorway comprises a two-tier façade of Corinthian columns topped off with a pedimented roofline supporting a Cross. Inside, there is a series of large pillared side altars, enlivened with gilded *trompe l'œil* mosaics by the Spanish-born artist Gaetano Garcia. Over the main altar, Saint Ignatius is shown rising on a cloud up to Heaven, where the Trinity wait to greet him with an immortal crown.

The neighbouring Jesuit College (Isusovački samostan) was founded before the church in 1658. Planned as early as 1558 by one of the first Jesuits, Nicholas Bobadilla (1511–1590), it was only realised later due to the Jesuits' persistent anti-Islamic stance, which at the time conflicted with that of more tolerant Ragusans, who believed Ottoman suzerainty had its advantages. The college, in which the Renaissance poet Ivan Gundulić (1589–1638) was educated, was destroyed by the earthquake of 1667. Rebuilt in 1725 as the Collegium Ragusinum, which can be seen today, it was here that the respected polymath Ruđer Bošković (1711–1787) was educated. After the dissolution of the Jesuits in 1773, the college served as a military hospital and a seminary, and is now a Catholic secondary school.

The Baroque Church of St. Ignatius (Crkva sv. Ignacija) and some of its famous steps

The final element of Dubrovnik's finest Baroque ensemble is the Jesuit Steps. Completed in 1738, they were designed by Roman architect Pietro Passalacqua (1690–1748) and modelled directly on the Spanish Steps, which had been completed thirteen years earlier. They are a wholly un-Ragusan feature insomuch as their width and sweep are a luxury in a city constricted by its girdle of walls, where space comes at a premium. Both the steps and the square in front of the church serve as atmospheric venues during the annual Dubrovnik Summer Festival.

Other locations nearby: 10, 11, 12, 14

14 Remnants of the Romanesque

Old Town (South of Stradun), a short tour of Romanesque buildings, including the ruined Church of St. Stephen (Crkva sv. Stjepana) at the end of Ulica Stulina (note: the ruins are visible all hours)

In 1667, a great earthquake hit Ragusa. It levelled many of the city's elegant Gothic–Renaissance buildings built from the 14th-century onwards. The sheer quantity of architecture from the period, however, meant that some buildings survived and others were restored. Unfortunately that cannot be said of the city's earlier and less prolific stone architecture, namely religious buildings in the Romanesque and Byzantine style. From these remote periods, not nearly so much remains.

Naturally the city's Romanesque remnants are slightly more numerous than their older Byzantine predecessors. As with the tour of Byzantine fragments detailed elsewhere in this book, the search for remains begins with the Cathedral (see no. 17). Nothing Romanesque remains above ground today but archaeologists have revealed subterranean evidence of two earlier iterations of the building, including a 12th-century Romanesque basilica that was also toppled by the 1667 earthquake. Travellers considered it "la piu bella in Illyrico" (the most beautiful in Illyria) on the basis of its high quality sculptures, several thousand fragments of which have been discovered, displaying a close connection between Ragusa and artistic centres in Apulia. One of the excavated walls was found to have been inscribed with several *graffiti* of ships, the earliest known depictions of sailing vessels in the city.

The tiny Romanesque Church of St. James (*Crkva sv. Jakov*) is best seen from the City Walls

Today, Dubrovnik has just one intact purely Romanesque building. The tiny, single-nave Church of St. James (*Crkva sv. Jakov*) is tucked immediately inside the north-eastern city wall, on Peline ulica. Its weather-worn, pan-tiled roof and apse can only be seen from the wall above. Unfortunately, down at pavement level the encroachment of other structures means that only part of the southern façade, with its

blind dwarf arcades, remains visible. The church is first documented in 1225, when it was built for the Dominican order, which had recently settled in the neighbourhood (they eventually built the huge monastery that today stands nearby) (see no. 30). The church's spartan interior features a 15th-century painting of the Virgin and Child by an unknown artist.

Until a few years ago, the Church of St. James was the single Romanesque building worth tracking down. The only other example was an unmarked jumble of ruins concealed behind a boarded-up doorway at the end of Ulica Stulina. They were all that remained of the Church of St. Stephen (Crkva sv. Stjepana), and most passers-by were unaware that this was once one of the city's most important buildings (it explains, for example, the naming of the important St. Stephen (Sv. Stjepan) Bastion on nearby Ulica Ispod Mira, as well as the adjacent doorway over which is carved Vrata S. Stjepana (St. Stephen's Gate). Fortunately the tantalising ruins, which lie within one of the oldest parts of Old Town, have recently been consolidated and can now be viewed through a grille. Beneath the ground, the footings of a tri-partite structure of the 8th- to 10th-centuries, with an apse at the eastern end, have been identified (see no. 17). Later, in the 11th-century, the building received an early-Romanesque upgrade in the form of a western extension, and later still, during the 12th- and 13th-centuries a Romanesque extension was added eastwards, including a new and larger apse. It is the remains of these Romanesque upgrades that are visible today.

Other locations nearby: 11, 12, 16

15 Ships and Sailors

Old Town (South of Stradun), the Maritime Museum (Pomorski muzej) in Fort St. John (Tvrdava sv. Ivana)

Between the 14th- and 18th-centuries, Ragusa was the capital of a tiny but influential aristocratic maritime republic. It operated one of the world's finest merchant fleets, its skilled captains helping create the wealth that financed the city's grand buildings. To discover more visit the Maritime Museum (Pomorski muzej) at Fort St. John (Tvrđava sv. Ivana). The setting is perfect, with the fort perched on the southeast side of the city's sea wall, where once it guarded the Old Port (Stara Luka).

The present fort is the result of several upgrades to the original 14th-century Dock Fort and its neighbour, Fort Gundulić. By 1500 the semi-circular bastion had been added to the former and the angular bastion to the latter. During the 1550s the various parts were merged into a single fortification according to existing plans by the Republic's municipal engineer, Paskoje Miličević (1440–1516).

Today, the Maritime Museum takes up two floors of the old fort. On the ground floor there are artefacts, documents, charts and navigational aids illustrating Ragusa's 16th-century heyday, one forged diligently through trading relationships established up and down the Adriatic coast, whilst under the alternating suzerainty of Byzantium, France, Venice, Hungary, Spain and Turkey. Key to this process was shipbuilding and in this Ragusa excelled. With over 180 large ships in the mid-16th-century, the Ragusan fleet rivalled that of Venice. Also on display are intricate models of Ragusan merchant ships, known as *argosies*, a name derived from the Italian *ragusea*, meaning a large three- or four-masted Ragusan-built carrack. With a small crew and largo cargo capacity, they were ideal for navigating the European coastline.

Up on the first floor, Ragusa's later maritime history is illustrated. Already by the closing years of the 16th-century, the Republic was losing its grip on the Mediterranean, as caravans began favouring Split for offloading, and England and Holland opened new shipping routes. The dissolution of the Republic under Napoleon made matters worse, and by 1880 the local building of sailing vessels had given way to the import of steam-powered vessels from Britain. Models and paintings of these craft, which necessitated the opening of a new deeper port at Gruž, are displayed.

Looking out from the fort over the Old Port, one sees two breakwaters. The Porporela directly beneath the fort is a quay built in 1873 by the Austrians. It has a light at its tip, as well as a wind compass engraved with a tribute to Dubrovnik's traditional seafarers: *Znanje, Vjera, Srčanost* (Knowledge, Faith, Prowess). Out in the bay is the Kaše, an island breakwater built perpendicular to the land. In the days of the Republic, enemy vessels were prevented from entering the port by means of a heavy chain strung between this breakwater and Fort St. John.

Beyond the Kaše are the St. Luke (Sv. Luka) Bastion and the stand-

A ship's wheel and two engine order telegraphs in the Maritime Museum (Pomorski muzej)

alone Fort Revelin (Tvrđava Revelin), which guarded the opposite side of the port and the eastern approach to the city respectively. Looking landwards can be seen the Old Arsenal, a triple-arched structure in which argosies and other vessels were once built (see no. 19). In front are two piers, the Great Fishmarket Pier and the Small Pier, with bollards of Egyptian granite.

The maritime theme continues beneath the museum, with an aquarium *(akvari)* stocked with fish native to the Adriatic, and outside at Ulica kneza Damjana Jude 6, with the Miho Pracat Seamen's Club. Founded in 1953, this is one of Old Town's last uncommercialised bars and is filled with photos of ships and other nautical memorabilia.

Other locations nearby: 16, 17

16 The Pustijerne Palaces

**Old Town (South of Stradun), a tour of old palaces
in the Pustijerne district, including the Sorkočević (Bishop's)
Palace at Poljana Marina Držića 3**

The first iteration of Ragusa as a coherent settlement took shape during the 6th- and 7th-centuries. It occupied the south-western highpoint of what was originally an islet separated from the mainland by a marshy channel. Before the channel was infilled to enable Ragusa to spread onto the mainland, the settlement expanded westwards into the area known as Na Andriji, and then eastwards into the area between the cathedral and Fort St. John (Tvrdava sv. Ivana). This latter area was called Pustijerne from the Latin 'post terra' because at the time it lay 'outside the town'.

It was here during the 16th-century that a series of palaces were built for the Ragusan aristocracy. They are rendered in a typically Ragusan fusion of Gothic and Renaissance styles, including features such as Venetian-style balconies, large hooded windows, and neo-Classical doorways emblazoned with family escutcheons. Spared the worst of the damage wrought by the great earthquake of 1667, the palaces make for an interesting thematic tour.

The tour begins just behind the cathedral at Poljana Marina Držića 3. Here stands the former palace of the Sorkočević (Sorgo) family, their coat of arms displayed over the doorway (alternative Italian surnames such as Sorgo were often used by the Ragusan nobility). The family arrived in Ragusa from Albania in 1272 as grain-traders and were ennobled soon after for introducing the edible grain *sorghum* during a period of famine. They subsequently became wealthy ship-owners.

Built in the early 16th-century, the original Sorkočević Palace was predominantly Renaissance in style, with Gothic elements deployed to emphasize the family's class and lineage, notably around the windows on the showy first floor *piano nobile* (similar styling can be seen in the familys's summer palace in the Rijeka Dubrovačka, see no. 43). Following the earthquake, the palace was given a Baroque makeover by Italian architect Tommaso Napoli (1659–1725) and occupied thereafter by Luka Sorkočević (1734–1789), Croatia's first symphonist, who committed suicide here. Later still, during the 19th-century, it became the property of the Bishop of Dubrovnik. Rendered uninhabitable in 1979 by another earthquake, the building has since undergone thorough restoration and is now open to visitors as the Sorkočević

(Bishop's) Palace. Highlights include a unique Renaissance gilded ceiling, Baroque illusionist frescoes, and a balcony *(empora)* cut through into the neighbouring church.

Now walk south to Restićeva ulica 1, and the former home of wealthy mariner and merchant Vice Stjepović-Skočibuha (1534–1588). A commoner from the isle of Šipan, he worked his way up from ship's scribe to become the most respected merchant of the day but refused the Republic's offer of ennoblement because it would not extend to his children. His palace, completed in 1533, is rendered entirely in the Renaissance style by the renowned Andrijić family firm of stonemasons creating a building just as grand as its aristocratic neighbours. As with the Sponza Palace (Palača Sponza), which the

A unique Renaissance ceiling in the Sorkočević (Bishop's) Palace on Poljana Marina Držića

family also designed, they followed the plans of a visiting Italian architect (see no. 23).

Now continue along Ulica od Pustijerne and turn right onto Ulica Brače Andrijića (named after the aforementioned masons). At number 10 there is the currently-abandoned former home of the Ranjina (Ragno) family, their escutcheon carved with three spiders representing the Italian version of their name.

More escutcheons adorn the next street along, Bandureva ulica, including those of the Bunić (Bona) and Kaboga (Caboga) families. Between them they produced two famous Ragusan envoys *(poklisari)*, Nikolika Bunić and Marojica Kaboga, who brought tribute to the sultan in Constantinople during the time Ragusa was under Ottoman suzerainty.

Other locations nearby: 11, 14, 15, 17

17 Byzantine Fragments

Old Town (South of Stradun), a short tour of Byzantine remains, including the Chapel of St. Cosmas and Damian (Crkva sv. Kuzmi e Damjana) at Poljana Marina Držića 3

Between the sixth-century and the turn of the first millennium, Dubrovnik was a rocky islet under the suzerainty of the Byzantine Empire. During this early medieval period, local bishops, with support from Constantinople, set out to evangelise the pagan Slavic (Croat) hinterland. Today, however, there are few visible reminders that Dubrovnik ever looked eastwards towards Byzantium.

The most obvious trace is Mount Srđ above the city. Its name is derived from that of the 4th-century Roman soldier Saint Sergius, who was martyred in Syria for his faith and subsequently revered in the Byzantine Empire as a protector of armed forces. As for domestic buildings from the period there are none. Being made of timber they were destroyed in 1296 during a great fire. Religious buildings, on the other hand, were made from stone and of these some tantalising fragments remain.

Byzantine window detail at the Chapel of St. Cosmas and Damian (Crkva sv. Kuzmi e Damjana)

The first stop is Dubrovnik Cathedral (see no. 11). Although there is nothing Byzantine above ground today, archaeologists have unearthed the shadowy 7th-century remains of a large, triple-naved basilica, including a crypt and some tantalising wall paintings showing just the feet and vestment hems of saints (see the plans pinned to the inside of the cathedral door). Lost to seismic activity, this building was replaced during the 12th-century with a Romanesque basilica (see no. 14).

Fortunately the next stop is tangible. The Chapel of St. Cosmas and Damian (Crkva sv. Kuzmi e Damjana) leans up against the Sorkočević (Bishop's) Palace at Poljana Marina Držića 3 (see no. 16). The façade incorporates an ornate limestone window, reused from some late-10th century structure. The jambs display finely-cut vegetal scrolling, edged on the inside with braiding known as *pleter*, and topped with a lintel of leaf stems. Although the work is typical of pre-Romanesque Croatian art, it shows a clear stylistic nod to Byzantine stone ornament.

Another Byzantine-era decorative detail hides not far away on the corner of Ulica Josipa Jurja Strossmayera and Crijevićeva ulica. Again a window, it consists of a slab of fine limestone pierced with ten circular apertures. It illuminates the crypt of the late-9th/early-10th century Church of St. Peter the Great (Crkva sv. Petra Velikog). Toppled during the great earthquake of 1667, it was only re-discovered in the 1960s beneath the concert hall of the Luka Sorkočević Art School (Umjetnička Škola Sorkočevića) (see no. 3). Some historians believe it was Dubrovnik's first cathedral.

Another rare Byzantine detail at the Church of St. Peter the Great (Crkva sv. Petra Velikog)

The final stop on this short tour is the ruined Church of St. Stephen (Crkva sv. Stjepana) at the end of Ulica Stulina (see no. 14). Excavations here have revealed evidence of a tri-partite building of the 9th/10th-centuries, with an apse at the eastern end. The Byzantine Emperor Constantine VII Porphyrogenitus (905–959) mentions it by name in his *De Administrando Imperio* (On the Governance of the Empire), and in 971 it was here that Saint Blaise (Sveti Blaž) appeared in a priest's vision warning of an impending Venetian attack (see no. 21).

It is worth noting that the reason these ancient fragments are clustered together is because this area – farthest from the mainland and closest to the sea – was one of the first parts of the town to be built and fortified. Emperor Constantine referred to such early medieval districts as *Sexteria* and by the 10th-century there were several here.

> Fragments from all these pre-Romanesque buildings have been brought together in a superb gallery of early medieval sculpture on the ground floor of Fort Revelin (Tvrđava Revelin) (see no. 31). They include a stone baldachin *(ciborium)* from the church of St. Peter and a delicate lattice screen *(transenna)* from the Church of St. Stephen.

Other locations nearby: 11, 15, 16, 18

18 History in the Rector's Palace

Old Town (South of Stradun), the Rector's Palace (Knežev dvor)
at Ulica Pred Dvorom 3

Ragusa during the time of the Republic was governed by a Great and Small Council, and an annually-elected Senate. Their titular head was a so-called *knez*. Meaning literally 'prince', though generally translated as 'rector', he had to be at least fifty years old in accordance with the State Statute and to hail from an aristocratic family. Elected by members of the Great Council, the position could only be held for a month at a time in order to prevent corruption. By 1808, when the Republic was abolished, Ragusa had seen no less than 5,366 rectors!

Each *knez* lived and worked in the Rector's Palace (Knežev dvor) at Ulica Pred Dvorom 3 (Old Town). The building unusually includes elements of all three architectural styles prevalent during its time as the Republic's administrative seat. This reflects not only the long life of the building but also its many functions, including as a gunpowder magazine, which exploded on two occasions and necessitated rebuilding in the style fashionable at the time. This explains why the original Venetian Gothic windows designed by Neapolitan architect Onofrio della Cava were later complemented by a Renaissance arcade and side windows by the Florentine Michelozzo Michelozzi (1396–1472). Later still, the great earthquake of 1667 prompted the installation of a dramatic Baroque staircase.

The entrance to the palace contains two interesting inscriptions. One of them – *Obliti privatorum publica curate* (Forget private concerns, think of the public good) – was there to remind each newly elected *knez* that his primary purpose was to serve the voiceless public and not himself. The other states erroneously that Aesculapius, the Graeco-Roman god of medicine, was born in Dubrovnik. Locals wittingly or otherwise conflated Epidaurus, the god's supposed Greek birthplace, with Epidaurum (modern Cavtat), the Roman settlement whence their ancestors originated.

The heart of the palace is an impressive atrium, which gave access to a variety of spaces: a notary's office, where citizens could request legal advice, a smart first-floor courtroom, and a grim dungeon in the basement. The Rector's state apartments were also on the first floor, where his study hung in red silk contains *The Baptism of Christ* by Mihajlo Hamzić (1482–1518), a member of the respected Ragusan School (see no. 30). In one of the arches of the atrium there is a bronze bust of wealthy Lopud-born shipowner Miho Pracat (1522–1607). He was the only commoner ever memorialised by the Republic, a tribute normally reserved for saints and supernatural beings. The atrium today makes a perfect setting for musical recitals during the annual Dubrovnik Summer Festival (see no. 31).

The Rector's Palace is home to Dubrovnik's Cultural History Museum (Kultur nopovijesni muzej). The oldest artefacts on display confirm that a settlement of Christian Illyrians existed on the site of Old Town as far back as the 6th-century. Don't miss the portrait of Saint Blaise (Sveti Blaž), half original and half overpainted, the keys to Old Town's two main gates, which were in the Rector's safekeeping, and the original 15th-century clock jacks from the bell

Croatian Tricolours flutter outside the Rector's Palace (Knežev dvor) on Ulica Pred Dvorom

tower (Zvonik) at the end of Stradun, the oldest such figures in Europe. There are also treasure chests with intricate locking mechanisms, coins and pocket watches, navigational aids, embroidery and weapons, as well as religious art and portraits of rectors. The 18th-century sedan chairs were used by the wives of Ragusan nobles.

After leaving the building, note the shrapnel marks on the side wall of the building, evidence of the ferocity of the Siege of Dubrovnik (1991–1992) during the Croatian War.

Other locations nearby: 17, 19, 20, 21, 22, 23

19 Of Argosies and Actors

**Old Town (South of Stradun), the Marin Držić Theatre
(Kazalište Marina Držića) on Ulica Pred Dvorom
(note: for current productions visit www.kmd.hr)**

Ragusa during the Renaissance period was a vibrant centre of the arts. Works by renowned playwright Marin Držić (1508–1567) and poet Ivan Gundulić (1589–1638) were performed in the fashionable salons of the capital Zagreb. In Ragusa, improvised stages were set up by amateur companies outside the Rector's Palace (Knežev dvor), in noble court-yards, and on the streets. Then, in 1612, Europe's first indoor public theatre opened on the Croatian island of Hvar. It was not until 1682, however, that Ragusa received its own indoor stage.

This first theatre might never have been established were it not for the great earthquake of 1667. One of the many buildings affected was the Arsenal, or *Orsan* as it was known to locals. Overlooking the Old Port (Stara Luka) and documented as early as 1272, it was here that merchant ships known as *argosies* and defence galleys were built. Extended during the late-15th-century by Paskoje Miličević (1440–1516), the Republic's municipal engineer, it consisted originally of four arched docks based on the Arsenale di Venezia (see no. 15). Following the earthquake, the Arsenal was relocated to Gruž and the old building became vacant. Now reduced to three docks and closed-off to the sea, it was here that Dubrovnik's first theatre opened, with a performance of the tragicomedy *Vučistrah* by Korčulan writer Petar Kanavelić (1637–1719).

With the abolition of the Ragusan Republic in 1808, the city's Great Council lost its function. Its former Chambers located behind the Arsenal, alongside the Rector's Palace (Knežev dvor) on Ulica Pred Dvorom, became the new Rector's Theatre. This was used until 1816, when it was destroyed by fire. As a result the theatre moved again, this time to a space in the nearby Gučetić (Gozze) palace, where it remained until 1864 (see no. 48). Only then was Dubrovnik's first purpose-built theatre erected back on Ulica Pred Dvorom between the Rector's Palace and a part of the old Arsenal that had become the Gradska Kavarna café.

Financed by nobleman Marin Luko Bondić (1812–1874), who had been ennobled by the then-ruling Austrians, the theatre was initially known as the Bondić Theatre. It operated under this name until 1944, when it became a branch of the newly-founded Dubrovnik National

The magnificent Marin Držić Theatre (Kazalište Marina Držića) hides behind a modest façade

Theatre. Later, in 1967, it was rebranded the Marin Držić Theatre (Kazalište Marina Držića) in honour of the 400th anniversary of the death of Ragusa's greatest playwright (see no. 5).

The theatre was designed in neo-Renaissance style by the architect Emil Vecchietti (1830–1901), who designed a similar theatre for his hometown of Split. Although the building gives nothing away from the outside, its Italianate interior is spacious, consisting of a stage, ground floor seating, and three tiers of boxes. The ceiling was painted in 1901 by the Cavtat-born artist Vlaho Bukovac (1855–1922) (see no. 34). Entitled *Dual Coronation in Heaven and on Earth*, it shows the goddess of poetry crowning Dubrovnik poets in heaven, whilst simultaneously crowning the notion of folk poetry as represented by a blind *gusle* player on earth. The stage curtain decorated in 2008 with motifs of Dubrovnik life is the work of contemporary artist Matko Trebotić (b. 1935).

As part of a major reconstruction in 1989, a 70-seat 'black box' stage was added to the theatre. Known as the Bursa Theatre, this simple, flexible space is used for small-scale productions that require minimal set decoration. Between them, the two stages offer a diverse repertoire, with an emphasis on works reflecting Dubrovnik's rich theatrical heritage.

Other locations nearby: 18, 20, 21, 22, 23

20 Cravats from Croatia

Old Town (South of Stradun), the Croata Museum Concept Store at Ulica Pred Dvorom 2

Walk along Old Town's Stradun and the streets running off it and it is striking how many premises have been given over to restaurants, fast food and gift shops. Fortunately in amongst them there are still a few real shops doing their best to provide Dubrovnik with a more authentic commercial landscape.

A fine example is the Croata Museum Concept Store at Ulica Pred Dvorom 2. One might easily pass it by were it not for the unusual door handle in the form of a neck tie, inscribed with curious symbols. Go inside and there is a mannequin draped with a beige neck tie, accompanied by an information panel explaining that the Cavtat-born artist Vlaho Bukovac (1855–1922) always wore something similar (another panel explains that Ragusan poet Ivan Gundulić (1589–1638) favoured a black tie). The reason for so much history is because the neck tie is a Croatian invention.

The Croata Museum Concept Store celebrates the Croatian invention of the neck tie

Its origin goes back to the 16th-century, when a knotted scarf worn for reasons of hygiene and cleanliness became an element of Croatian traditional dress. Later, during the Thirty Years' War (1618–1648), members of the Croatian Light Cavalry, known as Croats, reached Paris, where they were recruited as mercenaries into the French army of Louis XIV (1638–1715). As well as their distinctive fur hats and long red coats, they wore knotted scarves around their necks (lace and coarse linen for privates; silk and cotton for officers). French soldiers wore stiff high collars and were duly impressed by both the practicality and the elegance of the Croats' scarves. As a result, they and the fashion-conscious Parisians began wearing scarves *à la manière Croate*, corrupting the name to *cravat* in the process.

The Croata Museum Concept Store specialises in fine quality Croatian neck ties *(kravate)*, scarves and pocket squares for men and women. What sets them apart from other manufacturers is that many of the patterns used are related to Croatian history and culture. These include folk embroidery, architectural braiding (known as *pleter*), ancient Glagolitic script (as seen on the shop's door handle), and human fingerprints. Who knew that a Croatian, Ivan Vučetić (1858–1925), is credited with the invention of dactyloscopy whereby criminals are identified by their unique fingerprints?

On October 18th each year, Croatia celebrates its invention of the neck tie with a special Cravat Day (Dan Kravate). In Dubrovnik, some of Old Town's famous monuments are draped with huge neck ties, including Orlando's Column and the statue of Ivan Gundulić in the square outside the shop.

A few other idiosyncratic shops can be found within walking distance of the Croata Museum Concept Store. Algebra at Stradun 9, for example, is a bookshop with a good selection of Croatian history titles and travel guides. For antiques and collectibles visit Antiques Tezoro at Između Polača 13. For works by local artists try Homa at Boškovićeva 3, Artur at Ulica od Domina 2, and Art Gallery Talir at Čubranovićeva ulica 7. Terra Croatica at Ulica Od Puča 17 offers locally-produced salt, truffles, olives and honey. They also stock *Bajadera* nougat praline bars in their distinctive brown-and-yellow sunburst wrappers, made since 1911 by Zagreb company Kraš. Kraš also manufacture the ever-popular chocolate-topped Domaćica ('housewife') biscuits. In an effort not to be seen as sexist, the company briefly appended the names of various professions, including *menadjerica* (female manager) and *pravnica* (female lawyer), to the product's name and not surprisingly created an online stir in the process.

Other locations nearby: 9, 10, 18, 19, 21, 22

21 A Church for Saint Blaise

**Old Town (South of Stradun), the Church of St. Blaise
(Crkva sv. Blaž) on Luža Ulica**

Since the Middle Ages, Dubrovnik's patron and protector has been Saint Blaise (Sveti Blaž). A 3rd-century Armenian bishop beheaded for his Christian faith, he is identified by medieval Slavs with the pagan god Veles (hence his alternative name of Saint Vlaho). The image of Blaise can be found throughout Old Town and he still enjoys a well-attended annual festival enshrined in the city's earliest legislation dating from 1190.

Dubrovnik's chroniclers attributed the veneration of Saint Blaise to a vision witnessed in 971 AD by a priest at the ancient Church of St. Stephen (Crkva sv. Stjepana) on Ulica Stulina (Old Town) (see nos. 14, 17). It warned of an impending attack by the Venetians, who had dropped anchor offshore, ostensibly to take on water but secretly to assess the Ragusan defences. Blaise appeared as an old man with a long beard and a bishop's mitre and staff, and it is in this guise that he subsequently appeared on statues, coins, cannon and the state seal.

A good place to connect with Saint Blaise is in his church on Luža Ulica, at the east end of Stradun (Old Town). Commissioned by the Ragusan Senate to replace a 14th-century Romanesque church damaged by the great earthquake of 1667, it was completed in 1715 to a design by Venetian architect and sculptor Marino Gropelli (1662–1728). The new church, which was modelled on the Church of San Maurizio in Venice, is unusual in that it is oriented north–south due to limitations of space. The frontage is divided into four by Corinthian half columns supporting a neo-Classical pediment topped with three statues: Saint Blaise in the middle, with Faith and Hope on either side.

Inside, the church has a ground plan in the shape of a Greek cross, comprising a square nave, an oblong central cupola on more Corinthian columns, and an apse flanked by two sacristies. It has a barrel-vaulted ceiling and an ornate Main Altar in the Venetian Baroque style, which is worked in white and polychrome marble, with a niche high above containing a 15th-century silver statue of Saint Blaise. The statue, which miraculously survived the destruction of the earlier church, holds a model of pre-earthquake Ragusa in its hand.

The stained glass windows by modern artist Ivo Dulčić (1922–2006) depict various scenes from the Festival of Saint Blaise. They depict, on the left, the Rector releasing a dove, and on the right, a pro-

A stained glass depiction of the Festival of Saint Blaise

cession carrying the saint's relics, including his head and hands (see no. 11). The festivities commence on 3rd February, when churchgoers in traditional dress carry parish banners through the city accompanied by the Dubrovnik Musket-bearing Guard of Honour (Dubrovački trombunjeri). Should you miss it, head over to the nearby Sorkočević Palace at Poljana Marina Držića 3, where a unique film of the 1972 festival can be viewed.

Although the church does not hold the relics of Saint Blaise, which are in the Cathedral, it does contain the allegedly incorruptible body of 4th-century martyr Saint Silvan, which arrived from Rome in 1847. His head is thrown back to reveal the bloody gash on his neck that killed him.

The Ragusan Republic once boasted several colonies, the most unexpected of which was the town of Gandaulim in the Indian state of Goa. Whilst some commentators question the veracity of its existence, others point to the fact that Ragusa was involved in the global spice trade. How else could the presence of a church dedicated to Saint Blaise (São Brás) so far away be explained?

Other locations nearby: 9, 10, 18, 19, 20, 22

22 Orlando's Column

For over six centuries, Orlando's Column (Orlandov stup) has stood in the square in front of the Church of St. Blaise (Crkva sv. Blaža). There it has served a variety of purposes from being a place of punishment to more recently a photo opportunity for passing tourists. To understand its origin one must go back to the time of Charlemagne (747–814), the Frankish emperor who conquered, unified and ruled much of Europe.

According to legend, one of the twelve foremost knights (paladins) of Charlemagne's court was Roland. As military governor of Brittany, he was responsible for defending the Frankish frontier against the Bretons. Legend also states that during the 9th-century, Roland led a campaign to defend Ragusa against Saracen invaders. This, however, is chronologically impossible since the one historical attestation of Roland states that he was killed by Basques in 778 at the Battle of Roncevaux Pass in revenge for Charlemagne's destruction of Pamplona.

Exactly how the Roland story in Spain morphed a century later into that of Ragusa's Orlando is interesting. During the intervening years, the story of Roland's bravery was recounted by wandering minstrels. In their retelling, the Basques became Saracens and in this form the story permeated the history of many a free town across the Holy Roman Empire, where it served to highlight the benefits of imperial protection over governance by local nobility. Monuments to Roland were erected in some of these towns, most famously Bremen in 1404. In France, Roland became a central figure in *La Matière de France*, a cycle of medieval poetry akin to Arthurian legend, and in Italy he became Orlando, the main protagonist of *Orlando Furioso*, an epic work by Italian poet Ludovico Ariosto (1474–1533).

The monument in Dubrovnik does not date from the reign of Charlemagne. It was erected in 1418 by Italian-born Gothic sculptor and architect Bonino da Milano (d. 1429) (a study of the ground beneath the column revealed a slot suggesting that a wooden *carrus* or pillory post originally occupied the site). And rather than celebrating the benefits of imperial protection, the column's purpose here was to hark back to another Carolingian habit, namely that of deploying Roland's image as a legal symbol of the autonomy of a town's government. This legality was enforced by the presence of Durandal, Orlando's indestructible sword, which, according to legend, he hurled at the moment of his death into a poisoned river, thereby preventing it from falling into the hands of the enemy.

During the heyday of the Ragusan Republic, the steps of Orlando's Column were used as a podium from which new laws were proclaimed: mundane ones from the bottom step and more important ones from higher up. Thieves were chained here to serve public penance, and condemned men displayed as a deterrent to would-be lawbreakers. Later still, when Napoleon's dominance in the area was on the wane, Ragusa reasserted its independence by flying her famous *Libertas* banner from the column. Today the area surrounding the column is the setting for the opening ceremony of the annual Dubrovnik Summer Festival.

Orlando's Column (Orlandov stup) has long stood before the Church of St. Blaise (Crkva sv. Blaža)

Finally, notice the faint horizontal line etched into the step immediately beneath Orlando's feet. It is said to represent the length of Orlando's forearm from wrist to fingertip. This distance of exactly 51.2 centimetres served as the standard Ragusan unit of length, the *lakat*, and the line on the step once served as an official reference upon which local tradespeople could rely.

Other locations nearby: 18, 19, 20, 21, 22, 23

23 The Statute of State

Old Town (North of Stradun), the Sponza Palace
(Palača Sponza) at Stradun 2

The 16th-century Sponza Palace (Palača Sponza) is something of an oddity. Located at the east end of Stradun, Old Town's main arterial thoroughfare, it was never a palace in the residential sense of the word and instead served a variety of public functions. Moreover, it is the only palatial structure of the many that once lined Stradun to have survived the great earthquake of 1667. Its unusual name, derived from the Latin word *spongia* (meaning 'sponge') reflects the fact that rainwater from the roof of its 14th-century predecessor was collected for public consumption (see no. 2).

Rectangular in plan, with a central atrium, today's palace was built between 1516 and 1522 to a design by the Republic's municipal engineer, Paskoje Miličević (1440–1516). It represents the finest example of the Gothic-Renaissance transitional style deployed in many of Ragusa's pre-earthquake palaces. Thus we find at pavement level a six-columned Renaissance arcade, which conceals what remains of the original 14th-century building behind it. On the first floor, a Renaissance tripartite loggia sits between Venetian Gothic ogee windows, and at the top there is a row of Renaissance windows separated by a statue of Ragusa's patron and protector, Saint Blaise (Sveti Blaž). All elements were crafted by the Andrijić family firm of stonemasons from Korčula.

During the time of the Ragusan Republic, the Sponza Palace would have been a very busy place indeed. The ground floor rooms in both incarnations of the building served as a Customs' House, hence the alternative name *Divona*, a word derived from the Italian *dogana* (meaning 'customs'), which is hammered in nails together with the Ragusan crest on the main door. Merchant caravans heading out to (and returning from) the Balkan interior would come here to have their cargoes examined and the amount of duty payable calculated. As an assurance of trustworthiness and a warning against cheating, an inscription in the atrium reads: *Fallere nostra vetant et falli pondera. Meque pondero cum merces ponderat ipse deus* (Our weights do not permit cheating. When I measure goods, God measures with me). The doors leading off the atrium, each carved with a saint's name, led to bonded warehouse space.

The first floor was used by the Academia dei Concordi, a literary academy, where poets recited their latest works and scientists pro-

The word 'Dogana' on the Sponza Palace recalls the building's function as a customs' house

pounded their latest theories. Meanwhile, up on the second floor, the State Mint struck the Republic's currency – *perperae, grossi* and *ducats* – under the watchful eye of the Rector and a small board of directors drawn from the Ragusan Senate.

The Sponza Palace continued in its role as a customs' house right up until the early-20th-century, when it became a Museum of the Socialist Revolution. Today, the atrium is a public exhibition space, with the Dubrovnik State Archives (Državni arhiv u Dubrovniku) on the first floor. Its public reading room, which is open by appointment, is filled with documents, manuscripts, shipping records and cargo lists dating back to 1022. Pride of place goes to the city's original State Statute (1272) in which many political, criminal and mercantile laws were enshrined for the first time. It stipulated, for example, that no political decisions could be made when the southerly *Jugo* wind blew; that Rectors should reign only for one month to prevent corruption; that non-religious statues be prohibited in Old Town's public spaces; and that people only make honey and vinegar for personal use.

Like the nearby Rector's Palace (Knežev dvor), the Sponza Palace also serves as a performance venue during the annual Dubrovnik Summer Festival.

Other locations nearby: 19, 21, 22, 24, 25, 30

24 At Lući's Bar

Old Town (North of Stradun), a selection of bars, including
Caffe Bar Libertina at Zlatarska ulica 3 (note: Caffe Bar
Libertina is only open between 10am and 2pm daily)

Dubrovnik's has many bars but few could be described as idiosyncratic. One that passes muster is Caffe Bar Libertina. Tucked away on Zlatarska ulica, a narrow side street running north off busy Stradun, this old school establishment is known locally as Lući's after its laconic proprietor, Luciano 'Lući' Capurso. His claim to fame is being a former member of local folk-pop band Dubrovački trubaduri (Dubrovnik Troubadours), whose catchy song *Jedan Dan* (One Day) was the Yugoslavian entry at the 1968 Eurovision Song Contest (they achieved joint 7th position with Belgium and Monaco). His tiny bar with its vaulted ceiling is just as it should be: dark, smoke-stained and cluttered with ephemera and celebrity photos. Note the yellowing band photos in one corner, and the large rusty bell salvaged from one of Dubrovnik's old trams. Outside there is little to give the place away beyond a couple of chairs. This is the place to go if you want to drink coffee or something stronger with the *gospari* (literally 'nobles'), the word used to describe the true denizens of Dubrovnik. A recurring topic of conversation is football, including favourites, Hajduk Split. During the 1990s there were around 5,000 *gospari* living in Old Town but that number has dwindled to barely 500 today as properties have been given over to tourist lets. Lući's is perfectly complemented a few doors down by the lively studio of Igor Hajdarhodžić. Artist, actor and musician combined, he creates minutely-observed paintings in his own distinctive style, as well as quirky ship models made from discarded household objects.

Another decent local bar is Fontana not far away at Izmedju Polaca 5. With no real signage to speak of, realistic prices and affable bar tenders, it makes few concessions to the horrors of mass tourism and throws in a nautical theme for good measure.

Also north of Stradun is the Buzz Bar at Prijeko Ulica 21. This establishment offers a range of Croatian craft beers to discerning drinkers, including *Zmajska* from Zagreb, *Vunetovo* from Hvar and *San Servolo* from Istria. Hidden in plain sight, on a street usually associated with tourist trap restaurants, this is the place to kick back and enjoy some good beer, with live music at the weekends.

South of Stradun are Old Town's two famous Buža bars. Situated beyond holes *(Buža)* in the sea wall, these basic outdoor venues are

Lući Capurso runs one of the last real bars in Dubrovnik's Old Town

cut directly into the cliff face, with views directly out over the Adriatic. One is located at the corner of Ulica od Margarite and Grbava ulica, and the other can be accessed from near the junction of Ulica Ispod Mira and Pobijana ulica. The latter has the added attraction of a headland from which brave souls jump into the cerulean sea below.

Beyond Old Town in the district of Gruž is another idiosyncratic bar. The Cave Bar More can be found at Nika i Meda Pucića 13, or rather beneath it, since it occupies a natural cavern discovered during the construction of the Hotel More. It is set across three levels, allowing customers to admire this geological spectacle whilst enjoying their drink.

As well as Croatian craft beers, most bars dispense *Ožujsko* lager from Zagreb, as well as a variety of local spirits. These include *Rajika* (a grappa-like spirit with any number of flavours) and *Travarica* (pure grape brandy with an infusion of up to twenty herbs) (see no. 42).

Other locations nearby: 22, 23, 25, 30

25 The Jews of Dubrovnik

Old Town (North of Stradun), the Dubrovnik Synagogue (Dubrovačka sinagoga) at Žudioska ulica 5 (note: the synagogue can be visited independently or as part of a dedicated Jewish history tour at www.jewishdubrovnik.com)

Dubrovnik's Jewish community is the city's longest established religious minority, with a presence stretching back 700 years. In a city where *Libertas* (freedom) is cherished, the lack of systematic antisemitism is no surprise. During the time of the Republic, officials strove to attract Jewish business acumen without upsetting Catholic and other trading communities. That's not to say they didn't sometimes clash though.

The story of Dubrovnik's Jews goes back to 1326, when a Jewish physician was offered a job in the city. Although it is not recorded whether he accepted or not, more Jews followed and in 1352 they built a synagogue on Old Town's Žudioska ulica ('Jewish Street'). In 1407, the Ragusan Senate decreed that Jews be allowed to settle in Old Town, and a year later the synagogue was given legal status. This makes it the second oldest working synagogue in Europe after Prague.

The 1490s saw an influx of persecuted Sephardic Jews and Marannos (Jews forcibly converted to Christianity) from Spain and Portugal. This created tension with Ragusa's Catholic traders and in 1502 several Jews were wrongly charged with ritual murder and burned at the stake. The situation worsened and in 1515, the entire community was expelled.

The Jews returned in 1532, and this time settled outside Old Town's Ploče Gate (Vrata od Ploča). There they remained until 1546, when they were allowed back inside the city walls and occupied a gated ghetto centred on Žudioska ulica, where each Jew paid a rent. As the community grew, so did the ghetto, and in 1652 the synagogue relocated to the second floor of a town house at Žudioska ulica 5. There were still unpleasant incidents though. In 1724, for example, Jewish sacred texts were burned to cover up the fact that certain members of the Ragusan nobility were reading books forbidden to Catholics (in truth works on the French Reformation!). Again, in 1755, in the face of Ragusa's economic decline, Jews were excluded from commercial activity despite the fact that by this time they were co-owners of Ragusan ships and had established the Republic's first maritime insurance company.

With the French occupation of Ragusa in 1806, the Jews gained full legal equality and they opened a new burial ground at Boninovo (see no. 39). The arrival of the Austrians, however, in 1815, saw equality withdrawn and Jewish prosperity waned. Equality was only reinstated under Croatian law in the mid-19th-century, when the predominantly Sephardic community was bolstered by members of the Ashkenazim. Since then Dubrovnik's Jewish community has dwindled, including during the Second World War, when the occupying Italians interned them and twenty seven ended up in Nazi extermination camps.

An ornate torah finial in the Dubrovnik Synagogue (Dubrovačka sinagoga)

These days Dubrovnik's Synagogue (Dubrovačka sinagoga) is as much a museum as a place of worship. A narrow flight of stairs takes visitors up to the sanctuary, its striking blue ceiling decorated with tiny white Stars of David. Big enough to hold the 260 members recorded at the community's peak in 1830 (but now used by barely 40), it is divided in two by an arched partition. Women occupy a raised gallery on the south wall, while men sit on high-backed chairs along the north and south walls. From the raised eight-sided platform (or *bimah*) the Torah is read and then stored away in the Ark *(aron kodesh)* beneath a draped baldachin. The small museum contains old Torah scrolls and ornate Torah finials, silk Torah mantles, Ark curtains *(parochets)*, prayer shawls, and a list of those Jews murdered during the Holocaust.

Other locations nearby: 21, 22, 23, 24

26 The Art of Conflict

Old Town (North of Stradun), War Photo Limited at Antuninska ulica 6

Were it not for the occasional shrapnel mark on the paving slabs of Stradun or the cabinet of exploded missiles at the Franciscan Monastery (Franjevaāki samostan), one could imagine that conflict had not visited Dubrovnik since the Second World War. On the contrary, the city was heavily shelled in the early 1990s during the Croatian War (see nos. 32, 40). Remarkably by 1999 most traces of the damage wrought on Old Town had been repaired. As with conflicts elsewhere, however, the painful memories lingered and in 2003 a unique gallery was established to illustrate why.

War Photo Limited at Antuninska 6 (Old Town) is the work of Wade Goddard (b. 1969), a photographer who travelled from New Zealand to cover the violent breakup of Yugoslavia. So affected was he that rather than heading home afterwards he stayed on in Croatia, initially in Zagreb and then later in Dubrovnik. His aim in establishing the gallery was to deploy conflict images as a means of hammering home the raw violence of armed conflict and its aftermath, as well as the deadly myth of its appeal. Goddard could easily have limited the scope of his gallery to his own experiences in Croatia. Instead and much to his credit he expanded its remit to encompass works by fellow photographers from global war zones past and present.

The gallery is spread across two floors. The first floor hosts temporary exhibitions devoted to specific conflicts and particular photographers. The images, all beautifully mounted and lit against dark walls, range from the horrific to the poignant and the absurd. Each has been chosen for its ability to convey an unbiased, non-political message with a human element. Undoubtedly disturbing at times, the images speak clearly to visitors of all ages – from schoolchildren to adults – of the intolerance and nationalistic idealisms that lead to (and so often perpetuate) conflict.

On the second floor are two permanent displays. One called *The End of Yugoslavia* documents the bloody disintegration of the country, including not only the siege of Dubrovnik but also events elsewhere in the Balkans, including Kosovo, and Bosnia and Herzegovina. The photographers whose work is represented include American photojournalist Ron Haviv (b. 1965), French photographer Alexandra Boulat (1962–2007), Zagreb-born Darko Bandić (b. 1967), Danish photojour-

Peter Northall's photo of a damaged Dubrovnik building is displayed at War Photo Limited

nalist Jan Grarup (b. 1968), Reuter's editor Yannis Behrakis (1960–2019), the Bosnian Ziyah Gafic (b. 1980), and British photographer Peter Northall (b. 1958). Wade Goddard's own images are given space, too, illustrating his time in Mostar covering the war in Bosnia. It is sobering to think that similar scenes were played out not so long ago on the now-peaceful streets surrounding the War Photo Limited gallery.

Also on the second floor is the gallery's Limited Edition Print Room. On display are high quality, numbered copies of photos taken by renowned war photographers for the world's leading media organisations. Printed using archival inks and signed by the photographers, each can be purchased as part of a limited edition print run.

There will always be a war raging somewhere in the world. War Photo Limited serves to remind people of that, and to point out to them that the consequences, and the lessons, of war continue long after the fighting stops.

Other locations nearby: 6, 27, 28

27   A Beautiful Monastic Cloister

Old Town (North of Stradun), the Franciscan Monastery (Franjevaăki samostan) at Poljana Paska Miličevića 4

Many visitors begin their exploration of Old Town at the western Pile Gate (Vrata od Pila). Just inside it at Poljana Paska Miličevića 4 stands the Franciscan Monastery (Franjevaăki samostan). It contains not only Croatia's most beautiful cloister but also one of the world's oldest operational pharmacies.

According to legend, the monastery was founded after Saint Francis of Assisi (c. 1181–1226) visited Ragusa *en route* to the Holy Land to evangelise the Saracens (Muslims). Whatever the truth, the saint's followers – his Little Brothers *(Mala Braća)* – arrived in the early-13th century as part of a broader effort with the Dominicans to suppress the Balkan-based Bogomil heresy that threatened the Ragusan Church.

Initially, the mendicant Franciscans were not permitted to live inside the city walls and instead occupied a monastery outside the Pile Gate, where the Hilton Imperial now stands. Later, during the 14th-century, they were given land inside the gate, with instructions to guard it against intruders (the Dominicans likewise guarded the city's Ploče Gate (Vrata od Ploča) to the east).

Of the original Romanesque-Gothic monastery church, completed in 1317, little remains. Following the great earthquake of 1667, it was reworked in an Italianate Baroque idiom. What does survive is an early-15th century bell tower (Zvonik) and an almost life-sized Gothic *Pietà* (the Virgin Mary cradling the crucified Christ) above the church door (see back cover). The work of local stonemasons, it is clearly inspired by Venetian sculpture and includes a flanking figure holding a model of the pre-earthquake church.

Except for the stone pulpit, which also survived the earthquake, the church interior is Baroque, too. Features include a main altar surrounded by twisted marble columns, five elaborate side altars, and an organ loft adorned with musical *putti*. To the left of the altar is a stone slab marking the grave of celebrated Ragusan poet Ivan Gundulić (1589–1638) (see no. 10).

The real architectural highlight of the monastery is its beautiful Romanesque-Gothic cloister built around 1360. Designed by Montenegrin architect Mihoje Brajkov, each side of the cloister is divided into three *hexaphorae* (six-light bays) by pairs of slender, eight-sided columns (120 columns in all), crowned with decorative, humorous and sometimes grotesque capitals. Above each bay is a single large oculus. The cloister garden is planted with palms, box hedges, and pink and yellow roses.

At the entrance to the cloister is the monastery pharmacy. Founded in 1317, it is the world's third oldest working pharmacy after those in Padua and Baghdad. Originally used exclusively by the monks, it later became a public facility concocting all manner of remedies from flea deterrents to love potions. These days it sells regular pharmaceuticals, as well as skin preparations made using traditional recipes. Note the vintage advertising display for *Aspirin*.

The pharmacy was originally located in what

A detail of the beautiful cloister at the Franciscan Monastery (Franjevaäki samostan)

is now the monastery museum, where the fittings from its 16th-century incarnation are displayed, including mortars, pestles, scales and alembics for distillation. Also exhibited here is a 14th-century relic of Saint Ursula, a 15th-century silver thurible, a painting of Ragusa before the great earthquake, and sheet music written by Luka Sorkočević (1734–1789), the first Croatian symphonist.The monastery's 17th-century library, which contains several thousand valuable books and manuscripts, is unfortunately off-limits to visitors. Today just a handful of monks remain to watch over this magnificent legacy.

Just left of the monastery entrance there is a disused gargoyle (or *maskeron*). Visitors enjoy balancing on it because local folklore says this will bring them good luck!

Other locations nearby: 1, 2, 26, 28

28 Secrets in Small Churches

Old Town (North of Stradun), a tour of five small churches, including the Church of Sigurata (Crkva Sigurata) at Ulica od Sigurate 13

Dubrovnik's Old Town contains many small churches but they are often only visited by architecture buffs. This is a pity since most contain something worth seeing. What follows is a handful of them and the little secrets they contain.

First on the list is the well-hidden Church of the Transfiguration (Crkva Sigurata) at Ulica od Sigurate 13. Just look for the archway out of which is growing a fig tree. First documented in the 12th-century, the church received its current Baroque makeover following the great earthquake of 1667. Archaeologists have found evidence for two earlier smaller churches on the site dating from the 6th and 9th-centuries. Since the 13th-century, Franciscan nuns have had a convent here. Their museum, accessible from Ulica Celestina Medovića, contains a 14th-century processional Cross, 16th-century paintings, and various liturgical objects. There are also items used traditionally to support their order, including needlework equipment and a pair of 18th-century looms. Even if the church is closed, the courtyard in which it stands is one of the most tranquil Old Town has to offer.

Despite its strong female associations, the church was once the seat of Ragusa's Guild of Blacksmiths, which explains the gravestones decorated with hammer-and-anvils at the bottom of the broad steps. The Republic's Catholic craftsmen and other professions were organised into a system of twenty-one guilds or confraternities, each of which was based in a city church. Membership conferred social and commercial benefits, as well as a quasi-religious duty to promote piety and charity among the people.

The Ragusan guilds crop up again in the Church of All Saints (Crkva Svih Svetih) at Ulica od Puča 8. A stone tablet embedded in the façade is inscribed *Confratenità dei Muratori* (Guild of Stonemasons), with an emblem comprising various tools. The church was built in 1452 as the city's only triple-nave church with a rectangular apse. It too was damaged during the great earthquake and rebuilt in Baroque style. Inside is a 17th-century altarpiece by renowned Neapolitan painter Andrea Vaccaro (1604–1670).

Next up is the Church of St. Roch (Crkva sv. Roka), the patron saint of plague sufferers, at Ulica za Rokom 4. The curiosity here is not actually the church but rather a faint medieval Latin *graffito* outside, just beyond a blocked-up doorway opposite Ulica Zlatarićeva 7. It reads: *Pax. Vobis. Memento Mori Qui. Ludetis Pilla, 1597* (Peace be with you, remember you will die, you who play with ball). Clearly the words of a local driven to distraction by children playing ball! Alongside the church is the Kino Jadran, an *al fresco* cinema open during the warm summer nights.

The fourth small church is the Church of St. Luke (Crkva sv. Luka) at Ulica Svetog Dominika 4. Although it dates back to the 9th-century, the real treasure here is the late-15th century Gothic lunette over the door. Depicting three saints, it is the work of the renowned Petrović brothers, whose work also adorns the Dominican Monastery (see no. 30). The church is currently used as an art gallery.

The courtyard containing the Church of Sigurata (Crkva Sigurata) is worth visiting in its own right

The final church in this selection is the Church of Our Lady of Mt.Carmel (Crkva Gospe od Karmena) at Ulica za Karmenom 1. Completed in 1636, it is a fine example of early Baroque sacral architecture, with a splendid painted ceiling.

Dubrovnik's other guild churches include the carpenters' Church of St. Joseph (Crkva svetoga Josipa) and the Grenadiers' Church of St. Sebastian (Crkva sv. Sebastijana) in Old Town, and the shipbuilders' Church of St. Nicholas (Crkvica sv. Nikole) in Gruž.

Other locations nearby: 26, 27, 29

29 A Game of Thrones' Tour

Old Town (North of Stradun), a tour of locations used in the filming of Game of Thrones, including Fort Minčeta (Tvrđava Minčeta) at Ulica Ispod Minčete 9 (note: whilst these locations look wonderful on the small screen they are all the more engaging in real life as is the history behind them)

According to viewers and critics alike, one of the best fantasy television series of recent years has been *Game of Thrones*. This hugely popular drama based on the novels of George R. R. Martin (b. 1948) was created for American television network HBO, which premiered its eight seasons between 2011 and 2019. The show's huge success has spawned an active international fan base, with devotees travelling to the locations where filming took place.

Game of Thrones was shot in various parts of the world, including Canada, Iceland, Malta, Morocco, Spain, and the United Kingdom. But it is Croatia that many fans associate with the show's fictional world. Dubrovnik's fortified Old Town doubled perfectly as King's Landing, capital of the Seven Kingdoms of the continent of Westeros. One of the show's main story arcs concerns the Iron Throne of the Seven Kingdoms, which the noble families of Westeros seek to claim or else gain independence from.

To discover the real locations behind the fictional ones join a guided tour (www.dubrovnikgameofthronestour.com & www.kingslandingdubrovnik.com). Led by enthusiastic guides, the focus is set squarely on Season Two. Old Town's towering fortifications are particularly effective, including Fort Bokar (Tvrđava Bokar), which looks down from sea cliffs onto the Adriatic (the fictional Blackwater Bay) (see no. 1). Elsewhere, Fort Minčeta (Tvrđava Minčeta) at the top of Ulica Ispod Minčete doubles as the exterior of the House of Undying in the trading city of Qarth, where one of the main protagonists, Daenerys Targaryen, goes in search of her stolen dragons. In reality, the fort began in 1319 as a square fort. The decision in 1453 to strengthen Dubrovnik's north-facing landward flank from attack saw Florentine architect Michelozzo Michelozzi (1396–1472) wrap a sturdier cylindrical bastion around it, completed in 1461 by local stonemason Juraj Dalmatinac (1410–1473). In the late-15th century, the Republic's municipal engineer, Paskoje Miličević (1440–1516), added the crenelated crown. With walls almost 20 feet thick, the fort occupies the highest point of Old Town's fortifications.

Within Old Town, the tour takes in several locations, including the Rupe Ethnographic Museum (Ethnografic Museum Rupe), which doubles as Littlefinger's brothel, the Jesuit Steps (Skale od Jezuita), which are the setting for the Walk of Atonement performed by Cersei Lannister, and Ulica Svetog Dominika, along which various market scenes are set (see nos. 4, 13). The Rector's Palace (Knežev dvor), with its theatrical staircase, is used for the meeting of Daenerys and the Spice King in the city of Qarth (see no. 18).

More locations lie just outside Old Town. These include Pile Bay (Uvala Pile), where members of House Lannister bid farewell to Princess Myrcella Baratheon, after which they are attacked by an angry mob. The bay is also where Robert Baratheon's bastard sons are killed. Overlooking the

The colossal Fort Minčeta (Tvrđava *Minčeta*) guards Old Town's north-western corner

bay is Fort Lovrijenac (Tvrđava Lovrijenac), which doubles as the Red Keep, home of the evil King Joffrey, where a tournament is held in honour of his thirteenth name day (see no. 37). Nearby Gradac Park appears twice in Season 4 providing the setting for the Purple Wedding feast during which King Joffrey is poisoned, and for the scene in which Sansa flees from King's Landing (see no. 38).

Two further locations lie farther afield. The botanical gardens on the island of Lokrum, which also stand in for the city of Qarth, are where Daenerys Targaryen and her entourage attend a party (see no. 55). Farther up the coast, the Trsteno Arboretum doubles as the gardens of King's Landing, where several of the main protagonists hatch their plots (see no. 48).

Other locations nearby: 28

30 Glories of the Ragusan School

Old Town (North of Stradun), the Dominican Monastery and Museum (Dominikanski samostan i muzej) at Ulica svetog Dominika 4

Ragusa during the late 15th- and early 16th-centuries was a magnet for talented artists. So much so, that a distinct Ragusan School evolved. Several of the magnificent works created by its members are displayed in the Dominican Monastery and Museum (Dominikanski samostan i muzej) at Ulica svetog Dominika 4 (Old Town).

The Dominican Order came to Ragusa from Italy in 1225, part of a broader effort with the Franciscans to suppress the Balkan-centred Bogomil heresy. The location chosen was an important one, being just inside the eastern Ploče Gate (Vrata od Ploča). There, over the next two centuries, the Dominicans created an impressive monastic complex, with high outer walls, a red-roofed cloister and the Gothic Church of St. Dominic (Crkva sv. Dominik). The monastery is approached by a broad stone staircase, its balustrade half-blocked to protect the modesty of female visitors.

The final elements added to the complex during the 15th-century were the cloister, Capitulary Hall, and sacristy. Of these the cloister is a gem, its round Renaissance arches with Gothic-style *triphorae* (three-light bays) designed by a Florentine architect (note the rough-hewn troughs in the courtyard, which date from Napoleonic times, when the monastery served as a stable!). The vaulted Capitulary Hall in which the monks once debated now contains a painting of Mary Magdalene by Titian (c. 1488/90–1576), the leading light of the Venetian School, as well as the graves of various nobles and other worthies. The sacristy meanwhile was designed by the Republic's municipal engineer, Paskoje Miličević (1440–1516), who is buried there (see no. 23). The distinctive belfry was part-funded by the local Gundulić family but not completed until the 18th-century.

Alongside the Capitulary Hall there is a small monastery museum containing Ragusan gold jewellery and limb-shaped silver votive offerings. There are also several ecclesiastical works by members of the Ragusan School active during the transition from the Gothic period to the Renaissance. Three of them should be mentioned here.

The first, Nikola Božidarević (c. 1460–1517/1518), was born in Kotor, Montenegro and studied in Venice. Several of his works are displayed in the museum: a triptych showing Saint Blaise holding a model

Detail of a pedimented altarpiece by Ragusan master Nikola Božidarević

of the city before the great earthquake of 1667; the Annunciation beneath clouds of winged cherubs; and a beautiful pedimented altarpiece (see no. 38). When compared with the 14th-century gold altar Crucifix in the monastery church, with its paintings by the Venetian Paolo Veneziano (d. 1358), the influence of the Italo-Byzantine-style is clear.

The second artist, Lovro Dobričević (c. 1420–1478), also hailed from Kotor and studied in Venice. He specialised in painting icons and iconostases for Orthodox churches and monasteries in Bosnia-Herzegovina, as well as polyptychs in the Roman tradition in Ragusa. The Dominican Monastery holds his magnificent ten-panelled polyptych showing the *Baptism of Christ*, flanked by holy men.

The third artist is Mihajlo Hamzić (1482–1518). Born in Ston, he too studied in Italy before returning to Ragusa to practice his trade. Of only two surviving works, his altar triptych painted for the Lukarević family is on display. It shows Saint Nicholas flanked by various saints and again clearly shows the influence of Venetian painting. The rest of Hamzić's work, as with several other members of the Ragusan School, was lost in the great earthquake of 1667.

The church includes several modern works, including paintings by Vlaho Bukovac (1855–1922) and Đuro Pulitika (1922–2006), a statue by Ivan Meštrović (1883–1962), and a mosaic altarpiece by Ivo Dulčić (1916–1975) (see nos. 34, 47).

Other locations nearby: 31

31 The Musical Fortress

Old Town (North of Stradun), Fort Revelin (Tvrđava Revelin)
outside the Ploče Gate (Vrata od Ploča)

During the 15th- and 16th-centuries, the Ottoman Empire undertook a period of expansion courtesy of its adventurous sultans. Although Ragusa was a tributary of the Ottomans – in return for which she enjoyed free trade on Turkish soil – this didn't dissuade sultans from creeping steadily westwards. With this in mind the Ragusans set about safeguarding the eastern land approach to their city with a huge fortification called Fort Revelin (Tvrđava Revelin).

The name 'Revelin' derives from *rivelino* or *ravelin*, a term used in military architecture to describe a standalone fortification built opposite a city gate. Fort Revelin was built in 1462 outside Ragusa's eastern Ploče Gate (Vrata od Ploča). Initially little more than an earthen mound, by the 1530s it was clad in masonry by Italian architect Antonio Ferramolino (d. 1550) and had become the strongest element in the city's fortifications.

The fort takes the form of an irregular quadrilateral, its southern side sloping down to the sea, its other three sides surrounded by a deep ditch. A bridge on one side gives access from the fort to the Ploče Gate, whilst a second with a drawbridge leads out to the suburbs (both the work of the Republic's municipal engineer Paskoje Miličević (1440–1516)). The thick walls are pierced by embrasures in which guns were placed. The masonry was built so sturdily that the fort withstood the devastating great earthquake of 1667. So much so that in the earthquake's immediate aftermath Ragusa's Great Council held its sessions here, and the Cathedral treasures were stored for safekeeping. More than three centuries later, the fort sheltered Dubrovnik's citizens during the Croatian War (see no. 32).

Nowadays Fort Revelin remains perfectly intact but serves a very different purpose. The roof of the fort, which forms a vast stone terrace, doubles as a stage for the Dubrovnik Summer Festival held annually between July and August. Meanwhile, the interior of the fort, which comprises three huge vaulted spaces, hosts the lively Club Revelin, a night club that offers a variety of events, including raves and rock concerts. That the walls of the fort are so thick ensures that those living nearby are not too greatly disturbed!

Also on a musical note but a more restrained one, the Dubrovnik Symphony Orchestra (Dubrovački simfonijski orkestar) is based

The mighty Fort Revelin (Tvrđava Revelin) with its drawbridge (right) to the suburbs

here. It uses a three-storey building attached to the fort's west side as its rehearsal space, which explains the Classical music that sometimes hangs on the air. Known as *Slanica*, the building was originally Old Town's salt magazine, hence it being protected by a statue of Dubrovnik's patron Saint Blaise (Sveti Blaž).

The Dubrovnik Symphony Orchestra was established in 1925 although talented musical groups sponsored by the nobility are well-documented from the time of the Ragusan Republic. It staged its first concert in Old Town's Marin Držić Theatre (Kazalište Marina Držića) (see no. 5). Since then the orchestra has performed regularly at the Dubrovnik Summer Festival, as well as throughout Croatia and internationally. Its repertoire includes many home-grown 18th-century works, including those of composer Luka Sorkočević (1734–1789). Croatia's first symphonist, he was born into a distinguished aristocratic family and later served as Ragusa's ambassador to Vienna, where he was influenced by Joseph Haydn.

Although Dubrovnik has had a thriving archaeological society since the 1870s, it is currently without a dedicated archaeological museum. Until it gains one, a superb collection of early medieval sculpture is displayed on the ground floor of Fort Revelin, alongside the remains of a cannon foundry.

Other locations nearby: 30, 33

32   The View from Mount Srđ

The Suburbs (Ploče), a cable car (Uspinjača) ride from the base station at Ulica Kralja Petra Krešimira IV. 10A to the summit of Mount Srđ (Brdo Srđ) (note: the cable car only runs between April and October)

Between 1st October 1991 and 31st May 1992, during the time of the Croatian War, Serb forces laid siege to Dubrovnik. An estimated three thousand shells rained down on the historic city causing indiscriminate damage. It has been calculated that 72% of Old Town's buildings were damaged in the process. Remarkably by 1999 most of the damage had been repaired leaving little physical evidence that the conflict had ever occurred. From above, however, the picture was different. Many of the city's shattered old terracotta roofs received new red pantiles, and they still stand out today. One way of seeing them is by taking a cable car (Uspinjača) up to the viewing station at the top of Mount Srđ (Brdo Srđ).

The cable car is boarded at Ulica Kralja Petra Krešimira IV. 10A, just a couple of streets north of Old Town. From there it is a four minute ride to the top. On the way notice how the mountain side is largely bare. Once upon a time it was forested with holm oaks, which locals called *dubrava* from the old Slavic word *dub* meaning 'oak tree' (and from where the city received its modern name). These were felled long ago for use in house construction, whilst the pines that replaced them were felled during the war.

Mount Srđ, which forms part of the Dinaric Alps, rises to 1,350 feet above sea level. At its summit stands Fort Imperial completed in 1812 by the French General, Auguste de Marmont (1774–1852), when Dubrovnik formed part of the Napoleonic Kingdom of Italy. Its purpose was to defend the city's northern flank, which at the time stood on the border with the Ottoman Empire.

During the Croatian War, Mount Srđ saw some of the fiercest fighting as Serb forces backed by Montenegrin militias sought to bomb Dubrovnik into submission. Remarkably Croatian forces retained control of the old fort, which they kept supplied as French troops had before them by means of a zig-zag donkey path. The television mast on the summit, however, was destroyed by the Yugoslav Air Force, as was the cable car before the enemy retreated. These violent events are recorded in the Museum of the Homeland War (Muzej Domovinskog rata), which occupies Fort Imperial today and contains not only

The view of old Old Town from Mount Srđ (Brdo Srđ) is breathtaking

many poignant photos and film footage but also the tattered flag that flew over the fort during the fighting (it should be noted here that the term 'Homeland War' (Domovinski rat), as well as 'Greater-Serbian Aggression' (Velikosrpska agresija), are terms generally only used inside Croatia).

Looking out from the summit of Mount Srđ it is still easy to make out which buildings in Old Town were re-roofed as a result of the hostilities. Additionally Stradun, the Jesuit Steps (Skale od Jezuita), the Bell Tower (Zvonik), fountains and fortifications were all damaged and then restored to exacting UNESCO standards. That the restoration was carried out relatively quickly was because much of the necessary equipment was already in place as a result of an earthquake that struck Dubrovnik in 1979.

Dubrovnik's wartime destruction created two important precedents. Firstly, UNESCO sent delegates to the area to record and subsequently repair built fabric considered of world importance, in conjunction with local and national institutions. Secondly, the guilty verdicts received by the commanders of the Yugoslav People's Army (Jugoslovenska narodna armija) before a UN International Criminal Tribunal were the first convictions for crimes against cultural heritage in an international criminal proceeding.

33 The First State Quarantine

The Suburbs (Ploče), the former Lazareti Quarantine Infirmaries at Ulica Frana Supila 8–10

The foundation of the Ragusan Republic in 1358 and its early economic success brought with it enlightenment and the early adoption of modern institutions. These included the validation of Europe's first insurance law (1395), the abolition of slave trading (1416) and the world's first orphanage (1432). Even before the Republic, a sewage system (1296), medical service (1301), pharmacy (1317) and almshouse (1347) had all been established. Then, in 1378, the Republic initiated the world's first state-imposed quarantine policy.

During the mid-14th-century, a bubonic plague pandemic dubbed the Black Death swept across Europe. Ragusa was first exposed to it by the Mongols in 1348 as they fought their way across Europe. Despite many hundreds of people dying, Ragusa was eager to maintain its mercantile ascendancy. Still too small to survive a full lockdown, in 1377 Ragusan officials decided to permit trading so long as visitors quarantined beforehand.

Initially a quarantine of 40 days was required on uninhabited islands such as Mrkan, Supetar and Bobara (the word 'quarantino' is derived from the Italian word for a 40-day period, a length of time inspired by Biblical events such as Jesus' fast in the wilderness). During this time, everyone from merchants from the Ottoman Empire to ambassadors and even bishops, were supervised by guards, cleaners and, just in case, a gravedigger. Once 40 days had passed, they were allowed to come ashore to conduct their business.

The world's first custom-built quarantine hospital opened in Venice in 1423. A little later, in 1430, Ragusa inaugurated its first mainland quarantine station in the Franciscan Convent of St. Mary at Danče, just west of Old Town (see no. 38). Capacity, however, was limited there and so in 1590 the Ragusan Senate commissioned its own dedicated quarantine hospital immediately outside Old Town's eastern Ploče Gate (Vrata od Ploča).

Located at the intersection of important land and sea trade routes, the so-called Lazareti (literally 'infirmaries') were constructed between 1627 and 1647. They comprised ten large quarantine cells, each separated from the next by a gated inner courtyard looking out to sea. Recently restored, the complex is Europe's only intact early quarantine complex and rightly under UNESCO protection.

One of the courtyards at the former Lazareti Quarantine Infirmaries

Although the last outbreak of plague in Ragusa occurred in 1526, the Lazareti's usefulness continued in that in 1724 the complex was declared an integral part of the city walls. These days it has been repurposed as an arts and leisure complex (Lazareti kreativna cetvrt Dubrovnika), which provides a home for the Lindo Folklore Ensemble, Lero Student Theatre, Otok Gallery, Deša regional centre for community development, and the Lazareti Club.

It is just a pity that the Lazareti are without a museum. Instead, whilst exploring the various courtyards, bear in mind that novel tools designed to ensure social distancing were once used here, including poles with spikes on their tips. An early form of contactless payment consisted of a cash drawer with a hole cut in it, which enabled those incarcerated to still do some business without handling any money. And for those who broke quarantine severe punishment awaited, including torture, amputation of nose or ears, and even death.

It is interesting to compare the old Ragusan approach to a pandemic with that of Dubrovnik's current governing officials. Today it is tourism that is the lifeblood of Old Town, which explains why Dubrovnik was among the first European cities to re-open to vaccinated tourists during the recent Coronavirus pandemic, and why it campaigned hard to reinstate flights from America.

Other locations nearby: 30, 31, 34

34 Croatian Modern Art

The Suburbs (Ploče), the Museum of Modern Art Dubrovnik (Umjetnikča Galerija Dubrovnik) (MoMAD) at Ulica Frana Supila 23

Dubrovnik is all too easily defined by its medieval walls, Gothic-Renaissance palaces and Catholic churches. Such a definition, however, denies the city's significant contribution to modern art. To discover more one must stray beyond Old Town and visit the Museum of Modern Art Dubrovnik (Umjetnikča Galerija Dubrovnik) (MoMAD) at Ulica Frana Supila 23 (Ploče).

Founded in 1945, the museum is housed inside the former villa of shipping magnate Božo Banac (1883–1945). One of Dubrovnik's wealthiest citizens, he was educated in Britain before joining the Ivo Račić Transatlantic Company (Atlantska plovidba Ivo Račić). In 1924, he founded his own navigation company, Jugoslavensko-amerikanska plovidba, and four years later became the first foreign ship-owner to sit on the governing board of Lloyd's Register of Shipping in London. Success enabled him to commission prominent Croatian architects Lavoslav Horvat (1901–1989) and Harold Bilinić (1894–1984) to design his showcase villa. Completed in 1939, it is a cross between a Ragusan aristocratic summer residence and a sleek, space-conscious Modernist mansion.

In 1948, the villa was converted into a museum with the specific intention of collecting, studying and displaying Croatian art from the late-19th-century onwards. Almost 3,000 pieces have since been acquired through purchases and donations, including paintings and sculptures, graphic art, photographs, videos, and art installations.

The collection is spread across three floors and takes the form of seasonal and thematic exhibitions. The holdings from the period up until the end of the Second World War contain many works by artists related to Dubrovnik. The first Croatian Modernists, they include Cavtat-born Vlaho Bukovac (1855–1922), who combined *Belle Époque* romanticism with near photographic realism. He is also credited with introducing *plein-air* painting into Croatian art. Another, Mato Celestin Medović (1857–1920) from the Peljesac Peninsula, is remembered for his large-scale depictions of the Dalmatian coast. Also represented are works by Emanuel Vidović (1870–1953) and Mirko Rački (1879–1982), both of whom are associated with the city of Split.

The 1950s and 60s are represented by the revered triumvirate of

Ivo Dulčić (1916–1975), Antun Masle (1919–1967) and Đuro Pulitika (1922–2006). Connected by friendship and an affinity for the Colourist and Expressionist genres, their works are also displayed in the MoMad-administered Gallery Dulčić-Masle-Pulitika (Galerija Dulčić-Masle-Pulitika) at Poljana Marina Držića 1 (Old Town). Also included are works by local painters whose careers peaked in the 1970s and 80s, including Milovan Stanić (1929–1989), as well as younger painters working in the post-modernist idiom in the present century, such as Ivan Skvrce (b. 1980).

There are works by various influential Croatian art groups, too, including Exat 51, which specialised in geometric abstraction during the 1950s,

Adio by Vlaho Bukovac at the Museum of Modern Art Dubrovnik (MoMAD)

the avant-garde anti-art Gorgona in the 1960s, and New Tendencies in the 70s, part of the post-informel art movement.

As far as modern Croatian sculpture is concerned, there are pieces from the 20th-century onwards by the likes of Ivan Kožarić (1921–2020), Ksenija Kantoci (1909–1995) and Ivan Meštrović (1883–1962), whose *Distant Sounds* (1918) adorns the museum's atrium. Other sculptures are displayed on the villa's Grand Terrace.

Most recent of all are post-conceptual, digital and generative works by installation artist Slaven Tolj (b. 1964), video artist Alen Floričić (b. 1968), and performance artist Pasko Burđelez (b. 1969).

The former studio of Đuro Pulitika (Atelje Đure Pulitike) is preserved just as the artist left it adjacent to the Maritime Museum (Pomorski muzej) in Old Town's Fort St. John (Tvrdava sv. Ivana). That it is difficult to find means its creative atmosphere has been preserved.

Other locations nearby: 33

35 A Walk to Orsula Park

The Suburbs (Ploče), a walk out to Orsula Park (Park Orsula) on Ulica Frana Sulipa (note: it is a fairly strenuous half hour walk to reach Orsula Park from the Ploče Gate (Vrata od Ploča) and a bus service is available for the return journey if needed)

There are many wonderful views of Old Town from beyond the city walls: looking east from Park Gradac, for example, or south from Mount Srđ. Another is looking west from Orsula Park (Park Orsula) and the walk there reveals some less well-known local history.

The walk begins outside the Ploče Gate (Vrata od Ploča), where Ulica Frana Supila passes beneath the massive Fort Revelin (Tvrđava Revelin) (see no. 31). The suburb beyond was once the Tabor, the chief marketplace of the Ragusan caravan trade with the Balkans. This is where caravans of up to 300 mules offloaded produce from the fertile Konavle valley to the east, and where Muslims descending from Bosnia and Herzegovina via the frontier village of Brgat held a bazaar. Although the Turkish *hans* are long gone and the area built over, the monumental lion's head fountain used by the muleteers still gurgles behind the bus shelter.

From here Ulica Frana Supila follows the old trade route eastwards along the coast. On the right-hand side it passes the former Lazareti, Europe's only fully preserved quarantine complex, beyond which a stone staircase leads down to the ever-popular Banje Beach (Plaža Banje) (see no. 33). A little farther on, on the left, is the fortress-like Museum of Modern Art Dubrovnik (Umjetnikča Galerija Dubrovnik) followed thereafter by a series of impressive seaside hotels (see nos. 9, 34). One of them is the Hotel Grand Villa Argentina beyond which the road splits. To the right Ulica Vlaha Bukovca – named for the Cavtat-born artist Vlaho Bukovac (1855–1922) – passes the extraordinary Villa Sheherezade (Vila Šeherezada), a Moorish fantasy built in 1929 for a wealthy Estonian businessman and now an elite hotel. In the cliff face beneath the villa is Betina špilja, a sea cave popular with canoeists. The Ragusan scientist Marin Getaldić (1568–1626) conducted experiments here using parabolic mirrors to set enemy ships ablaze from afar!

Back on Ulica Vlaha Bukovca, proceed past the Hotel Villa Dubrovnik along the tree-shaded cliff-top to reach the neighbourhood of Višnjica. Here can be found the compact former Benedictine Monastery

Orsula Park's ruined Chapel of St. Ursula

and Church of St. James (Benediktinski samostan i Crkva sv. Jakova). Dating back to 1222, when it was founded by a member of the noble Gundulić family, this is where Ragusan emissaries paused during Ottoman times on their way to pay the Republic's annual tribute in Constantinople. Although the monastery was dissolved after the fall of the Republic, the church remains in use. A stairway behind the monastery leads down to Plaža Sveti Jakov, a rare sandy beach favoured by locals.

Shortly before the monastery, a concrete path leads steeply uphill to rejoin Ulica Frana Supila. From here it is not far to a signposted track leading upwards through forest to Orsula Park. Little more than a rugged hillside with footpaths, the park is named for the ruined 14th-century Chapel of St. Orsula. The chapel's attribution is connected to the cult of Saint Ursula, patron saint of virgins, because Ragusa's unhappy maidens are said to have once come here to throw themselves from the sea cliffs below.

Just above the chapel there is a 350-seat amphitheatre set into the hillside. As well as providing a magnificent vista back towards Old Town and out towards Lokrum island, the amphitheatre serves as a popular summer concert venue. The large building complex on the headland beneath the park is the Belvedere Hotel, abandoned in the early 1990s after being damaged during the Croatian War (see no. 45).

Other locations nearby: 36

36   Dining in a Konoba

Suburbs (Bosanka), a selection of traditional dining experiences, including Konoba Dubrava in Bosanka village (note: Bosanka is easily reached by car or taxi, or alternatively a strenuous walk up Put od Bosanke, with superb views back to Old Town)

Visitors to Dubrovnik will want to try authentic traditional Dalmatian cuisine. Prepared simply, its strength lies in the use of good quality ingredients sourced locally and seasonally. Other than adding parsley, garlic, olive oil and lemon, the inclusion of spices and elaborate sauces is rarely necessary. Grilled fish, seafood and baked lamb predominate, as well as Italian-inspired pasta and risotto, cured ham *(pršut)*, and cheese in oil *(skripavac)*. Meat and fish dishes are typically served with roast potatoes and Swiss chard *(blitva)*, and salads are plentiful in summer (replaced by shredded pickled cabbage in winter). For those with a sweet tooth there is crème caramel flavoured with rose liqueur *(rozata)*.

Dubrovnik boasts plenty of restaurants, including several that include the word *konoba* in their name. Originally meaning a room or shed in which food and wine was stored, a *konoba* is best equated with a tavern, where friends gather to eat, drink and make merry. South of Old Town there are two excellent *konobas*. Konoba Dubrava can be found in Bosanka village, which nestles among the pine trees on Mount Srđ. The speciality here is *Janjetina Ispod peke* (literally 'lamb under the bell'). This is a one-pot dish of lamb and rosemary potatoes *(krumpir s ružmarinom)* slow-cooked on live coals in a pot with an iron lid (pork, veal, octopus and even bread is cooked the same way). A staple of many a Croatian wedding, it needs booking at least three hours in advance. Other dishes on the menu include homemade beef soup, cold fish and meat platters, grilled minced meat fingers *(ćevapi)*, and homemade sour cherry and apple strudel.

Farther south, beyond Čilipi Airport, is Konoba Vinica Monkovic in Gruda. The setting here is as memorable as the food, which is served at tables perched on stilts above the fast-flowing River Ljuta. The wine comes from the adjacent vineyard.

Locals will rightly tell you that Old Town offers little in the way of decent traditional fare. It does, however, have a couple of acceptable *konobas* although they cannot compare with those in the country. Konoba Dundo Maroje at Kovačka ulica 1 (Old Town) is a well-

Lamb under the Bell (Janjetina Ispod peke) is a house speciality at Konoba Dubrava

reviewed example, with dishes including seafood platters, mushroom and truffle gnocchi, charcoal-grilled octopus, and chicken and courgette risotto. Another is Konoba Jezuite at Poljana Ruđera Boškovića 5, where meals are served in the magical atmosphere of a terrace alongside the Baroque Jesuit Church (see no. 13).

Other Old Town restaurants include Kopun at Poljana Ruđera Boškovića 7, with its namesake dish of a capon slow-baked for six hours, Lokanda Peskarija on Na Ponti, where the signature dish is Venetian-inspired black risotto (Crni Rižot) coloured with squid ink, and Zuzori at Ulica Cvijete Zuzorić, where Dalmatian fish, seafood and pasta dishes are given a modern twist.

This brief epicurean survey finishes with a fine dining recommendation. The Michelin-starred Restaurant 360 is located on Ulica Svetog Dominika near the Ploče Gate (Vrata od Ploča). This is the place to come for the best in modern Mediterranean cuisine, as well as one of the country's finest wine cellars. During the summer months, diners are served at tables set out on the St. Luke (Sv. Luka) Bastion, with splendid views over the Old Port (Stara Luka) below.

When the trinity of grilled fish, baked lamb and risotto wears thin, look out for other local dishes such as Šporke makarule (chunky pasta goulash), *Pašticada* (lean beef studded with garlic and bacon, and marinated in wine), and *Zelena maneštra* (smoked meat and cabbage stew).

Other locations nearby: 35

37 Dubrovnik's Gibraltar

The Suburbs (Pile), Fort Lovrijenac (Tvrđava Lovrijenac) on Ulica Skalini dr. Marka Foteza overlooking Pile Cove (Uvala Pile) (note: a ticket to the Dubrovnik City Walls (Dubrovačke gradske zidine) includes access to the fort)

It is clear why Fort Lovrijenac (Tvrđava Lovrijenac) is called 'Dubrovnik's Gibraltar'. Perched on a 120-foot-high crag outside the west wall of Old Town, the freestanding redoubt was built to guard both sea and land approaches on this side of the city. Above the gate is inscribed *Non Bene Pro Toto Libertas Venditur Auro* (Freedom should never be exchanged for gold), a reminder that such fortifications helped Ragusa to remain a free trading republic for four and a half centuries.

A scenic approach to the fort can be made from Ulica sv. Đurđa, a stepped passageway that runs off the square in front of Old Town's Pile Gate (Vrata od Pila). It opens out onto Pile Cove (Uvala Pile) from where a footpath (Ulica Skalini dr. Marka Foteza) winds up to the fort, passing some quaint rock-cut fishermen's huts along the way.

Legend maintains that during the 11th-century the Venetians planned to fortify the crag for themselves, and keep Ragusa firmly under their control. To prevent this, the Ragusans threw up a fort in just three months! Lovrijenac, however, is not officially documented until 1301, when Ragusa's Great Council voted on a 'Commander of the Fort'. Drawn from the local nobility, like Ragusan Rectors he only held the position for a month to prevent anyone from using the fort to foment anti-government activity. Today, the fort looks much as it did over 700 years ago. Triangular in plan, with two entrances with drawbridges, it has sturdy sea walls almost 40 feet thick.

During the 20th-century, the fort served two very different purposes. In the Second World War, when Dubrovnik was a part of the Independent State of Croatia (Nezavisna Država Hrvatska) (NDH), a puppet state of Nazi Germany and Fascist Italy, it served as a prison for so-called enemies of the state. It should not be forgotten that between 1941 and 1945, the NDH was run as a single-party state by the fascist ultranationalist Ustaša organisation. Led by Ante Pavelić (1889–1959), it waged a campaign of terror against Serbs, Jews, Roma and anti-Axis Croats and Bosniaks, and created a network of twenty concentration camps across Croatia.

Since 1950, the fort has been used more peaceably as an outdoor location for the annual Dubrovnik Summer Festival, which runs between

10th July and 25th August and includes classical music, theatre and opera. Performances of Shakespeare's *Hamlet* on the fort's roof are a popular and atmospheric fixture. The festival opens with a ceremony before Old Town's Church of St. Blaise (Crkva sv. Blaža) during which the flag of Dubrovnik is raised over Orlando's Column (Orlandov stup) and a recital of *Dubravka*, an ode to liberty by celebrated local poet Ivan Gundulić (1589–1638), stirs the hearts of patriotic Croatians (see nos. 10, 22). Other venues include Fort Revelin (Tvrđava Revelin), the Rector's Palace (Knežev dvor), and the Lazareti Quarantine Infirmaries (see nos. 18, 31, 33).

The brooding Fort Lovrijenac (Tvrđava Lovrijenac) occupies a crag west of Old Town

Those for whom the Dubrovnik Summer Festival is too stuffy should head instead to the up-and-coming port district of Gruž. There for three months between June and September an alternative festival is staged at the TUP arts' complex (see nos. 41, 42).

The antithesis of Fort Lovrijenac's brooding presence is surely the light-hearted Love Stories Museum at nearby Ulica od Tabakarije 2. The goal here is not only to document historical and mythical love stories, romance on the big screen and the world's greatest love songs but also to collect and display love messages and tokens from ordinary people around the globe.

Other locations nearby: 38

38 Franciscans and Austrians

The Suburbs (Pile), Gradac Park (Park Gradac) on Ulica don Frana Bulića, which runs off Ulica branitelja Dubrovnika

One of Dubrovnik's prettiest seaside spots is Danče Beach (Plaża Danče) at the end of Ulica don Frana Bulića (Pile). Despite being only fifteen minutes west of Old Town, it rarely gets overly busy and is a good spot for swimmers and sunbathers alike. The 'beach', which actually comprises natural rock outcrops and concrete platforms, sits at the southern end of a rugged cove set against a backdrop of cypress trees.

To only remain at the water's edge though would be a shame since there are two locations worth exploring up on the sea cliffs. The first is the Convent of Our Lady of Danče (Gospa od Danača). The red-tiled Franciscan complex, with its flower-filled garden, began life in 1457 as a chapel financed by public subscription. A clue to its original purpose is its location: situated well beyond the city walls, its incumbents tended a graveyard for paupers and executed criminals, on a site previously occupied by a lepers' colony. This extramural location also explains why the chapel served as Ragusa's first mainland quarantine station (see no. 33).

The conventual Church of St. Mary (Crkva sv. Marije) is entered through a portal with a tympanum of the Madonna carved by an anonymous local craftsman. Inside are two magnificent treasures of the Ragusan School: a high altar polyptych painted in 1465 by Lovro Dobričević (c. 1420–1478) and a side altar triptych painted in 1517 by Nikola Božidarević (c. 1460–1517/1518) (see no. 30). Both show the Madonna and Child centre stage, supported by various saints, including Saint Julian the Hospitaller, who is invoked by hospitals and leper colonies, and Saint Martin in whose sword is reflected a self-portrait of the artist.

At the top of the cliffs is Gradac Park (Park Gradac). It is sometimes called the 'Austrian Park' because it was laid out in 1897, when Dubrovnik was a part of the Habsburg Empire. During the park's heyday it was a fashionable place for well-dressed couples to promenade among the trees and eye-catching oddments of architectural sculpture. Much later it provided the same backdrop to a couple of episodes of the hit television series *Game of Thrones* (see no. 29). A path along the ridge at the top of the park offers views of Fort Lovrijenac (Tvrđava Lovrijenac) and Old Town to the east, and the Lapad peninsula to the

Sculptural fragments adorn the Austrian-era Gradac Park (Park Gradac)

west, a feature of which is the impressively terraced Rixos Hotel. Until just a few years ago, this was the concrete shell of the Hotel Libertas, which was bombed out by Serb forces in 1991 during the Croatian War (see no. 45).

Rather than returning along Ulica don Frana Bulića, look for Ulica Rudimira Rotera. This narrow stepped passage passes down one side a charming old palace, now a women's student dormitory. Note the slender stone pergola supports, which are a common feature of old Dubrovnik gardens.

It has been noted by Annabel Barber in her book *Visible Cities Dubrovnik* (Somerset, 2006), one of the first decent mainstream guides to the city, that in 1815, when Dubrovnik fell under the sway of Austria, the Ragusan ruling class stopped marrying, favouring extinction of their blood lines over life under foreign rule. Inevitably the old family names petered out and the last pure Ragusan aristocrat is thought to have died just after the Second World War. Their beautiful crumbling villas, however, can still be seen along Ulica branitelja Dubrovnika, the long road that connects Old Town with Gruž. It is a road worth walking despite it now being a busy one.

Other locations nearby: 37

39 Mortality and Modernism

The Suburbs (Boninovo), the Boninovo Cemetery (Groblje Boninovo) at Ulica Između tri Crkve 1

Until the establishment of the Boninovo Cemetery (Groblje Boninovo), Dubrovnik's first municipal burial ground, during the first half of the 19th-century, the city's majority Catholics were buried in churchyards and religious houses inside the city walls. In 1808, health concerns and a lack of space saw this practice banned by the occupying French. War and a lack of will, however, meant that a new extramural cemetery was not created immediately and instead people made do with the grave-yards of the Convent of Our Lady of Danče (Gospa od Danača), and the Church of St. Michael (Crkva sv. Mihajla) in the district of Lapad (see no. 38).

Dubrovnik's minority Jewish community was actually the first to secure land for burials outside the city walls in 1652 (see no. 25). They were also first to commence burials at the Boninovo Cemetery, when it finally opened in 1811. The land there had become available following the Russian-Montenegrin siege of Dubrovnik in 1806, when aristocratic summer villas in the area were destroyed by fire. In 1837 Dubrovnik's minority Orthodox Christian community followed suit (see no. 7). They secured what had been the garden of the Pozza Sorgo family's villa, its tree-lined central footpath retained as the main axis of the burial ground and the villa rebuilt to serve a funerary purpose.

Only between 1855 and 1860 did Dubrovnik's Catholics commence their own burials at Boninovo. Using land formerly owned by the Altesti family, again what had been a garden path became an axis and the villa rebuilt as a chapel. That a trio of sacred buildings now existed at Bononovo prompted the cemetery's central alley to be called Između tri crkve ('Between the Three Churches'). The various grave memori-als run the gamut of styles from neo-Classical to Modernist. Some give an idea of what the person did in life, for example that of a sailor in the form of an anchor inside a stylised ship's lantern, while others repre-sent well-known Dubrovnik families.

Finally, in 1935, a small area was carved out for members of the city's Muslim community, which represents the final extension of the cemetery as seen today. This last development nicely illustrates the changing demographics of Dubrovnik's population since up until the Second World War burials at Boninovo were predominantly Catholic. After the Second World War, management of the cemetery was removed from the various religious communities and transferred to a municipal utility company.

At the junction of Između tri Crkve and Ulica Ivana Matijaševića the melancholy mood lifts. Here can be found the Villa Rusalka, one of a trio of whitewashed villas designed by Nikola Dobrović (1897–1967), the Father of Adriatic Modernism. Born in Hungary and educated in Prague, Dobrović relocated to Dubrovnik in the 1930s intent on introducing modern architecture to the city. The Villa Rusalka completed in 1938 combines bold whitewashed forms outside and clean lines within, allowing the Mediterranean climate to permeate the house throughout. Notice the name and date perforated through the roof parapet, a trademark of Dobrović's work elsewhere. This includes

A sea captain's last resting place at Boninovo Cemetery (Groblje Boninovo)

the Villa Adonis at Trogirska ulica 4 (Srednji Kono) and the Villa Vesna on the island of Lopud, where his abandoned Grand Hotel can also be found (see no. 52). Completed in 1937, the hotel was the first reinforced concrete structure on the Dalmatian coast. Used to hold Jews during the Second World War, the hotel later became a Communist holiday facility and was subsequently closed.

Opposite the Villa Rusalka is the Slavica open-air cinema, which retains its huge Modernist concrete screen, installed when the cinema opened in 1958.

40 Relics of the Croatian War

The Suburbs (Batala), a tour of Croatian War relics and memorials, including the Sveti Vlaho naval vessel on Ulica Nikole Tesle

The death in 1980 of Josip Broz Tito (1892–1980), president and supreme military commander of the Socialist Federal Republic of Yugoslavia, triggered widespread geopolitical changes in the Balkans. Deepening ethnic tensions between the Croats and Slovenes on one side, and the politically dominant Serbs on the other, began tearing Yugoslavia apart. Then, in June 1991, Croatia declared independence. Until international recognition of the new Republic of Croatia a year later, Serb military forces aided by Montenegrin militias did everything to prevent it from happening. The Croatian War – known in Croatia as the Homeland War (Domovinski rat) – was the result.

During the course of the war, which lasted from 1991 until 1995, more than 430 Croatian military personnel from Dubrovnik were killed, the majority during the siege of the city between 1st October 1991 and 31st May 1992. Additionally, it has been calculated that more than 3,000 missiles landed on the town. Remarkably by 1999 most of the damage had been repaired leaving little evidence of the conflict beyond the starburst pockmarks on the paving slabs of Stradun, where enemy rockets exploded.

For those interested in the conflict there are half a dozen relics and memorials that make for a poignant thematic tour. The main memorial is the Museum of the Homeland War (Muzej Domovinskog rata), which occupies the Napoleonic-era Fort Imperial on the summit of Mount Srđ (see no. 32). Held by the Croatians in the face of fierce enemy attacks, the fort today houses a worthy permanent exhibition, with plenty of original artefacts. There are also three war memorials: a plaque attached to the fort reading "In memory of the Croatian defenders"; a large remembrance Cross; and a standalone monument dedicated to one Robert Isuvić of the defending 163 Brigade.

Two tangible relics of the war can be found in a park on Ulica Nikole Tesle overlooking Batala Bay (Uvala Batala). The first, at the junction with Hrvatskog Crvenog Kriza, is the *Sveti Vlaho*, a naval vessel of the Armed Boats Squadron Dubrovnik (Odred naoružanih brodova Dubrovnik). Established in 1991 as a volunteer unit of the Croatian Navy, its purpose was to transport troops, civilians and cargo during the Serbian blockade of the city. Sunk in late 1991, it was salvaged

The *Sveti Vlaho* is now a memorial to those lost during the Croatian war

a decade later and is now high and dry, and on permanent display (alongside it is a memorial to the citizens of Batala killed during the war). In 2006, the squadron was collectively decorated for the bravery of its members during the war. A little farther along the waterfront is a second military relic in the form of a camouflaged *Majsan* armoured vehicle. Built in the Inkobrod shipyard on Korčula, it too served in the defence of the city.

Several more memorials are dotted around the city. One on the railings of the Yacht Club Orsan on Ulica Ivana pl. Zajca (Babin Kuk) recalls four civilian sailors killed whilst trying to break through the Serbian blockade. Another in the form of a boulder can be seen at the ruined Strinćjera Castle (Tvrđava Strinčjera) on the hillside above Gruž. Three more consisting of simple stone plaques are located along the Rijeka Dubrovačka, north-east of Gruž: in the Sustjepan Cemetery; on Ulica uz Jadransku cestu in Mokošica; and on Ulica Bartola Kašića in Nova Mokošica.

This tour finishes back in Old Town where there is a memorial Room in the Sponza Palace (Palača Sponza) at Stradun 2 containing photographs of all those who died defending Dubrovnik.

41 The Red History Museum

The Suburbs (Gruž), the Red History Museum (Muzej crvene povijesti) at Svetog križa 3

In June 1991, Croatia formally declared independence and the dissolution of its association with Yugoslavia. This ended forty eight years of Socialist governance despite Serbian military efforts to prevent it (see no. 40, 45). In the quarter century since there has been much talk about the pros and cons of the country's Socialist experience but no public forum in which to address the matter. That changed in 2019 with the opening of the Red History Museum (Muzej crvene povijesti).

The museum is the work of a team of local creatives, including a historian, an architect, a designer, and a philosophy professor. Their aim is three-fold: to document daily life in Croatia during the Yugoslavian Communist period (1945–1991); to create a visitor attraction outside the well-trodden streets of Old Town; and to transform a former industrial concern into a cultural facility. The first goal has been achieved through the museum's lively mix of artefact-based commentaries and the recollections of real people, all brought to life in an immersive visitor experience. The latter two goals are fulfilled by the museum being located in the TUP arts' complex, a former Socialist-era Carbon Graphite Factory (Tvornica Ugljenografitnih Proizvoda) built in 1953 at Svetog križa 3, in the suburb of Gruž (see nos. 10, 42).

At the entrance to the museum, visitors can sit inside a red *Yugo* car, first manufactured in 1977 by Serbian manufacturer Crvena Zastava (Red Flag), and later exported around the world (see back cover). The exhibition space beyond is divided into three thematic sections. The first, *Socialism in Theory*, explains how the Yugoslav Communist Party was formed in 1919 but initially suppressed by the ruling royal government. In 1941, when Yugoslavia was invaded by the Axis powers, the Party's military wing, the Yugoslav Partisans, was instrumental in ousting them. In 1953, the Partisans' leader, Josip Broz Tito (1892–1980), became Prime Minister of the Federal People's Republic of Yugoslavia (later the Socialist Federal Republic of Yugoslavia). Under Tito, the Party was the first in the Eastern Bloc to openly oppose Moscow adopting instead a policy of independent Communism and workers' self-management known as 'Titoism'. The 'beloved' Tito's death unleashed latent ethnic tensions that led to the violent breakup of Yugoslavia.

The second exhibition space is called *Socialism in Practice* and reveals what everyday life was like in Socialist Yugoslavia. A reconstructed pre-1989 apartment is used to reveal Communist policy on topics as diverse as design and architecture, television commercials, sport, pop music and sex education. Yugoslavia was the only Communist country to take part in the Eurovision Song Contest and it also participated in Miss Universe, with Dubrovnik's Nikica Marinović (1947–2008) reaching second place in 1966.

A bust of Tito in the Red History Museum (Muzej crvene povijesti) in Gruž

The third space, *Dark Side of Socialism*, reveals the repressive side of Communism. There was censorship, political persecution, biased courts and compulsory nationalisation, with the feared State Security Administration, the UDBA (Uprava državne bezbednosti), deployed to keep people in line. Religion was not forbidden but neither was it encouraged, so the faithful kept their Bibles and crucifixes in the privacy of their bedrooms.

Before leaving the museum visit the café in the shabby factory courtyard and enjoy a Socialist-era Coke, or *Cockta* (1953), or a Fanta-inspired *Pipi* (1971). The museum shop sells mugs with the words *Where Yugo I go*.

Another example of converting an industrial space into a cultural facility is the studio of modern artist Dubravka Lošić. Located in the former Radeljević oil factory at Obala Stjepana Radića 2 (Gruž), it can be visited by appointment (www.dubravkalosic.com).

Other locations nearby: 42

42 The Dubrovnik Beer Company

The Suburbs (Gruž), a visit to the Dubrovnik Beer Company at Obala pape Ivana Pavla II 15 (note: brewery tours by appointment only at www.dubrovackapivovara.hr)

"Dubrovnik's leading brewery with a craft soul and plans for World domination!" So reads the home page of the Dubrovnik Beer Company. Such a mission statement sounds ambitious but this recently-established independent concern is already making waves on the region's brewing scene.

Despite Croatia being ranked 14th in the world by beer consumption per capita, the country does not have a long history of brewing. During antiquity and the Middle Ages, there are few references to brewing in the historical sources. This is in stark contrast to wine, which historians suggest may have been produced as early as the 6th-century by the ancient Illyrians (see no. 50).

The first commercial beer was *Osječko* brewed in 1697 in the eastern region of Slavonia. Brewing did not become more widespread, however, until the 18th-century, followed by industrialisation of the process a century later. The similar-sounding *Ožujsko* brewed in Zagreb hit the market in 1892 and is still the country's most popular beer (in second place is the 'national beer' *Karlovačko*). Since then, brewing in Croatia has emerged as a significant business, generating well in excess of 300 million Euros annually.

Despite the commercial pre-eminence of the Ragusan Republic, which traded everything from wool and wood to grain and gold, Dubrovnik only recently received its first commercial brewery. The Dubrovnik Beer Company was founded in 2017 by three "crazy enthusiasts" at Obala pape Ivana Pavla II 15 (Gruž). A century ago, salt from the northern Adriatic island of Pag was stored here, and under Communism the building formed part of a Carbon Graphite Factory (Tvornica Ugljenografitnih Proizvoda). It is now a part of the TUP arts' complex (see no. 41). The company has since gone from strength to strength, creating a series of successful draft and bottled beers for different palates.

To discover more about their work, it is recommended to take one of the popular hour-long brewery tours. Participants are guided through the brewing process step by step, explaining the types of yeast, hops and malt required for successful, small batch brewing, and revealing why some beer is dark in colour whilst others are light. The brewery currently produces around 20,000 litres of beer annually, which is shipped to over forty local bars and restaurants.

Naturally each tour finishes in the brewery Tap Room with a tasting of the company's four signature beers. Three of them are named after regional winds that were once so important to the Ragusan Republic's fleet. They are *Maestral* (lager named after a refreshing summer wind), *Fortunal* (pale ale named after a sudden gusting storm) and *Grego* (milk stout named after a strong winter wind, which is also known as the Bura). The fourth, *Goa*, is an IPA named in the belief that the small Indian state was once a Ragusan spice-trading outpost (see no. 21). As with wine tasting, it is interesting to

Tereza Čabrilo brings expertise and a smile to the Dubrovnik Beer Company in Gruž

savour each brew in turn, and in so doing to discern their different and sometimes surprising flavours – from citrus notes and floral aromas to a hint of chocolate.

Half a dozen limited and seasonal editions are also brewed, including *Runner* (another pale ale), *Malik* (a Porter), *Libertas 70* (a hoppy lager), and *Hazy* (a fruity New England-style pale ale brewed in collaboration with Old Town's Glam Café, a craft beer oasis at Palmotićeva ulica 5). The company's brewers claim that the taste of their beers uniquely captures the joy of living in Dubrovnik, namely its clement weather, unsullied nature and crystal-clear waters. Cheers!

Other locations nearby: 41

43 A Drowned River Valley

The Suburbs (Rijeka Dubrovačka), the Rijeka Dubrovačka sunken river valley (note: the head of the valley is easily reached with Bus 1A/1B from Pile Gate to Komolac)

Look at an atlas and it is immediately clear that the coastline of Croatia is indented. Indeed only Norway, with its many fjords, has a more serrated coastline. In Croatia's case it is because in the distant past the movement of the earth's tectonic plates created a series of peaks and troughs parallel to the coast. We know these today as the Dinaric Alps. When the coast was drowned in postglacial times, the troughs became sounds and the outlying peaks became chains of offshore islands (see no. 52). Geographers call such a formation a 'Dalmatian Coastline'.

A fine example of a drowned river valley is the Rijeka Dubrovačka, north of Gruž. Crossed at its mouth by the impressive Franjo Tuđman Bridge (Most dr. Franja Tuđmana), the drowned valley, called a *ria* by geographers, stretches inland for three miles (see no. 44). With the bridge now carrying traffic that formerly had to circumnavigate the valley to enter Dubrovnik, the Rijeka Dubrovačka has become a peaceful and beautiful area to explore.

The bus from Old Town's Pile Gate (Vrata od Pila) follows Batahovina ulica along the right-hand shore of the valley. Almost immediately the summer palace of the Bunić-Kaboga (Bona-Caboga) family (Ljetnikovac Bunić-Kaboga) will flash by on the right. It is a reminder that the valley was once a favourite summer getaway for the Ragusan nobility. As the bus continues eastwards notice further villas, some with their own chapel attached as was the custom.

Eventually the village of Komolac is reached at the head of the inlet, where one should alight from the bus. The area is dominated by the smart ACI Marina and another old Ragusan-era summer residence that belonged to the Sorkočević (Sorgo) family. Remains of its French-style *parterre* gardens, private fishponds and landing stage can still be seen, as can the elegant palace, which is reached by means of a broad stone staircase decorated with carved stone fruit baskets.

Beyond the marina, the road makes a broad curve before crossing the inlet at its narrowest point. Here on the right can be seen a stretch of beautiful blue-green river and a gushing waterfall. This is the River Ombla, which emerges above the falls from a spring in the hillside, and flows just beyond the falls into the Rijeka Dubrovačka. At a mere ninety-eight feet in length, it is one of the world's shortest rivers. It has provided Dubrovnik with excellent potable water since the 1430s, and very good water it is since before emerging it passes through a series of limestone caverns typical of so-called *karst* scenery, which purifies the water (see no. 2). The falls can be seen up close by entering the huge disused flour mill that stands crumbling alongside them.

From here one can continue around the inlet and onto Ulica Rožat Donji as far as the large 16th-century Franciscan monastery on the shoreline. Alternatively walk back along Tenturija ulica towards the marina, a really lovely riverside walk, with the hilltop Church of Our Lady (Crkva Velika Gospa) rising above the reeds. Before the marina, turn left to regain the main road from where the bus returns to Old Town. On the way back you might see an empty villa or

The Ombla Falls (Izvor Omble) at the head of the Rijeka Dubrovačka

two on the opposite shore. Their abandonment dates from the time of the French occupation of Dubrovnik in 1806, when Russian forces mounted a siege hoping to take the city. They were aided by Montenegrin bandits, who came down from the high ridge above Komolac and ransacked the noble homes.

Other locations nearby: 44

44 The Franjo Tuđman Bridge

**The Suburbs (Nuncijata), the Franjo Tuđman Bridge
(Most dr. Franja Tuđmana)**

Until fairly recently, road traffic arriving into Dubrovnik from the north-west had to circumnavigate the Rijeka Dubrovačka, a deeply indented coastal inlet (see no. 43). This all changed with the completion of the impressive Franjo Tuđman Bridge (Most dr. Franja Tuđmana). Now the D8 state road is carried directly across the inlet, slashing miles off the previous journey, unless the northerly *Bura* wind is blowing violently, in which case the old route must again be taken.

Designed in 1989 at the University of Zagreb, the 1,699 foot-long bridge is of the cable-stayed variety. That is the weight of the road deck is supported by a fan-like series of thirty eight steel cables running directly up and over a 464-foot high vertical A-shaped pylon embedded on the western shore (rungs inside the pylon enable workers to climb safely up to the top of the pylon for maintenance). Construction was entrusted to a Split-based engineering company, Konstruktor, and a German concern, Walter Bau AG, however, work was unavoidably halted in 1991 by the onset of the Croatian War. This explains why the bridge was not completed until April 2002. With a price tag of 252 million Croatian kuna (c. 33 million Euros), it is currently the most expensive bridge ever built in Croatia.

Right up to when the bridge opened to traffic in May 2002 there was confusion over its name. Hrvatske ceste, the Croatian state road company which financed construction, promoted the name Dubrovnik Bridge (Most Dubrovnik). The Mayor of Dubrovnik, Dubravka Šuica, however, requested that it be named for Franjo Tuđman (1922–1999), who did much to secure Croatia's independence from Yugoslavia and who served as First President. Only in 2004 was the name changed officially to the Franjo Tuđman Bridge.

It is no coincidence that the bridge makes landfall close to Dubrovnik's deep-water port of Gruž. Once a separate town, this has long been a busy spot, especially since the early-20th-century, when it served as an Austro-Hungarian naval facility. It has since become the city's main ferry and cruise ship terminal. Even before the arrival of today's big ships, Gruž was an important transport hub as it is where Dubrovnik's trains and trams once converged.

The train line to Dubrovnik was inaugurated during the 1890s as an extension of the Brod–Zenica–Sarajevo *Bosna Bahn*. It was built by the Austrians in the wake of the Berlin Congress (1878), which enabled them to oust the Turks in Bosnia–Herzegovina. The line had a gauge of 760 mm – the so-called Bosnian-gauge – which was laid extensively across territories of the Austro-Hungarian Empire. The original steam locomotive that ran on these rails did so twice a day and was called Ćiro. Although parts of the line were converted to standard gauge in the early 1970s, the spur to Dubrovnik remained unaltered and was closed in 1976 for financial reasons. Despite being an important city, Dubrovnik only ever had a modest terminal station, which still stands alongside the modern bus station (the outline of the letters spelling 'DUBROVNIK' remains just visible).

As for Dubrovnik's trams, they started running in 1910, again with Bosnian-gauge lines. Gruž

Looking up at the impressive Franjo Tuđman Bridge (Most dr. Franja Tuđmana)

was the main suburban terminus, with an extension as far as the Lapad Peninsula. Trams were eventually withdrawn in 1970 following a fatal accident, when a tramcar left the rails and crashed at the Pile Gate (Vrata od Pila) terminus. The route has since been taken up by buses.

Other locations nearby: 43

45 A Resort in Ruins

Farther Afield (Kupari), the ruined holiday resort of Kupari (note: Kupari can be reached by road or else by foot on the coastal path from Mlini and should only be explored with great care)

Five miles south of Old Town is one of the Dubrovnik area's more curious sights. Just off the busy D8, the Croatian leg of the Adriatic Highway, lies the seaside resort of Kupari – but the visitor won't find any guests there. Unlike Old Town, which was scrupulously restored after the Croatian War (1991–1995), Kupari's bombed-out hotels resemble something from a dystopian fantasy film (see nos. 32, 40).

This part of the Croatian coast has long traded on its scenic quality. In 1919, it was Kupari's turn, when a Czech investor built the Grand Hotel on the shoreline. At the time, Croatia had recently seceded from the doomed Austro-Hungarian Empire to become a part of the nascent Kingdom of Yugoslavia, and Czechoslovakia had become a sovereign state. The elegant architecture of the Grand, a confection of stuccoed brick with neo-Classical flourishes, was a reminder of the time both countries had spent under the Habsburgs.

Fast forward now to the 1960s and Croatia is part of the Socialist Federal Republic of Yugoslavia. Josip Broz Tito (1892–1980), the country's president and supreme military commander, earmarked Kupari's sandy bay as a holiday resort for members of the Yugoslav People's Army (Jugoslovenska narodna armija). As a result, over the next twenty years five, several huge hotels were thrown up, with almost 1500 beds for officers and their families.

Compared to the nostalgic stylings of the Grand, the new concrete hotels were largely functional. First up was the Goričina, which opened in 1962 with 160 beds. A year later the Pelegrin was built on the Dubrovnik side of the bay. Its 400-plus bedrooms are contained within an inverted Brutalist ziggurat designed by Sarajevo-born architect, David Finci (1931–2017). A series of ramps provided vehicular access to the various levels and a great staircase led directly from the lounge to the beach.

Next was the Kupari, built in 1978, which added another 550 beds. Situated alongside the Pelegrin, its hillside-hugging blocks echoed hotels thrown up along the Spanish Costas around the same time. Last on the scene was the Goričina II built in the early 1980s. Adding 350 more beds, it was a response to the fact that the Yugoslav government

The ruined holiday resort of Kupari

had opened up Kupari to foreign tourists. The bold red-painted porch and basement discotheque were indicative of the age.

Despite its popularity, Kupari's glory days were numbered. In 1991, the Serb-dominated Yugoslav People's Army attempted to scupper Croatia's bid for independence. During the war that followed, Kupari's empty hotels were guarded by a small Croatian police force. On October 4th 1991, Yugoslav naval vessels fired on the hotels and within three weeks Yugoslav troops had taken Kupari. Not until May 1992 did a counterattack return Croat forces but by then the damage was done.

Since the Croatian Army's departure in 2001 there have been several attempts to revive Kupari. Most recently, in 2016, a consortium of local investors received a 90-year lease on the site, where they plan to create a new high end resort. They will have to have deep pockets though because all the hotels, with the exception of the listed Grand, face demolition.

On a sea cliff just south of Old Town is another abandoned hotel. The luxury Belvedere opened in 1985 with over 200 rooms, a helipad and its own jetty. Just six years later, however, it too was attacked and since left to crumble. Bought at auction in 2014 by a Russian billionaire, plans are also afoot refurbish it.

Other locations nearby: 46

46 The Mills of Mlini

Farther Afield (Mlini), the village of Mlini (note: Mlini can be reached easily by car, bus, and taxi or water bus from Dubrovnik's Old Port (Stara Luka))

The Vrelo River and an old grindstone (right) recall Mlini's time as a milling centre

Five miles south-east of Old Town lies the village of Mlini, one of several coastal resorts in the Municipality of Župa Dubrovačka. Despite being far quieter than neighbouring Cavtat, Mlini was once of intrinsic importance to Dubrovnik. There was a time when the great fortified city depended on Mlini not only for its flour but sometimes even its water.

During the Middle Ages, Mlini was known by the Latin name Molina meaning 'mill'. 'Mlini' shares the same etymology bearing witness to the village's long history as a centre for milling. The reason is clear since the village sits at the foot of a valley down which flows the spring-fed Vrelo River. The earliest mention of a mill here dates from the 13th-century, and by the time of the Ragusan Republic there were a dozen or so in operation. Wheat grown in Albania, Apulia, Ukraine and even North Africa was ground here and shipped onwards as flour to

Dubrovnik. So important was Mlini in this respect that it warranted a mention in the Republic's State Statute (1272).

From 1897 onwards, the mills of Mlini ceased using the river to turn their grindstones and instead used electricity generated by a converted mill. Eventually though, as technology and transport improved, the mills were closed and today just one is left standing alongside a pretty stone footbridge. A pair of grindstones is preserved nearby beneath an enormous Oriental Plane tree planted in 1742. Also on display is a carved stone trough *(kamenica)* once used to store olive oil and a reminder that olives were processed here, too.

The river also provided another commodity vital to Ragusa. During the 15th-century, two ships regularly transported potable water there from Mlini, where it was sold on to well-to-do private consumers and the rest used to refill depleted public wells. Until the construction of Onofrio's Fountains in 1436, Dubrovnik's own water sources often ran dry in times of drought (see no. 2). Much later, in 1953, the stream was harnessed again for the Modernist hydroelectric power station that today overlooks the harbour (note the pylons on the hillside above).

According to local legend, Saint Hilarion (291–371), an anchorite and founder of Palestinian monasticism, killed a dragon on the coast of Mlini thereby freeing the area from paganism. This explains the parish Church of St. Hilarion (Crkva sv. Ilar) on the hillside. Founded as early as the 12th-century, it was rebuilt in the Baroque style after the great earthquake of 1667. Inside is a large 15th-century cross, all that remains from the original church fittings, and some modern wall paintings by local artist Bruno Stane Grill (1927–2012) depicting the quake (the church opens for Mass on Sunday at 10am). The undated and unattributed work *Obrezanje Gospodinovo* (The Circumcision of Our Lord) is a rare motif in sacred art. A smaller church dedicated in the 15th-century to St. Roch (Crkva sv. Roka) stands almost on the beach. Its altar painting of the saint is by Dubrovnik artist Mladen Pejaković (b. 1928).

In a secluded cove east of Mlini stands the ruined Bettera family summer villa, which can be seen from the water taxi. It was once frequented by renowned polymath Ruđer Bošković (1711–1787). He not only produced a precursor to atomic theory but also identified the lack of atmosphere on the Moon. Proud of being "a Dalmatian from Dubrovnik", he believed in a Divine Creator and has a research institute in Zagreb named in his honour.

Other locations nearby: 45

47 The Cavtat Mausoleum

Farther Afield (Cavtat), the Račić Mausoleum (Mauzolej Račić) in the Cemetery of St. Roch (Groblje sv. Roka) (note: Cavtat can be reached easily by car, bus, taxi or water bus from Dubrovnik's Old Port (Stara Luka))

The seaside town of Cavtat lies thirteen miles from Dubrovnik's Old Town. Situated between two bays, at the foot of the wooded Rat Peninsula, its easy-going waterfront is lined with restaurants. Aside from sitting directly under the flight path of nearby Čilipi Airport, it boasts traditional stone houses, cobbled streets and several interesting buildings.

Cavtat began as the Greek Classical city of Epidaurus. Romanised and renamed Epidaurum in the 1st-century BC by Emperor Augustus (63 BC–AD 14), legends claims it to be the birthplace of Aesculapius, god of medicine. Various buildings have been excavated on the western shore of the peninsula and in the bay to the north, with more beneath the sea, victims of ancient earthquakes. During the 7th-century, when the city was sacked by Slavic tribes, its inhabitants fled north along the coast and settled Ragusa. This explains why Epidaurum was eventually renamed Ragusa Vecchia (Old Ragusa).

Cavtat's palm-fringed harbour is book-ended by a pair of churches, that of St. Nicholas to the south and Our Lady of the Snows to the north. The latter is attached to a Franciscan monastery founded in 1484 that now serves a residential function. The monastery church is worth a visit for its early Renaissance paintings, as well as a medieval altarpiece of Saint Michael (1510), who is depicted simultaneously weighing souls and battling the devil. It is the only-known surviving work of Vicko Lovrin (d. 1517), son of renowned Venetian church painter Lovro Dobričević (1420–1478) (see nos. 27, 30, 38). Another highlight is a semi-circular painting over the chancel arch depicting the Madonna and Child gazing at Cavtat at dusk. It is the work of local artist Vlaho Bukovac (1855–1922), who was the first Croatian admitted to the Paris Salon (see no. 34). More of his work is displayed in his birthplace museum at Bukovčeva 5, where the walls carry decorative friezes he painted aged sixteen, and in the former Rector's Palace at Obala dr. Ante Starčevića 18, which contains a large canvas of a Cavtat carnival.

Crowning the Rat Peninsula, in a grove of solemn cypress and pine trees, is the town's Cemetery of St. Roch (Groblje sv. Roka). Its modest headstones are lorded over by the striking mausoleum of the wealthy Račić family (Mauzolej Račić). Ivo Račić (1845–1918), an energetic local shipowner, made the family fortune by founding the Ivo Račić Transatlantic Company (Atlantska plovidba Ivo Račić), which boasted fourteen oceangoing schooners. Despite their wealth, however, the family met with tragedy. Ivo's son Eduard and his fiancée succumbed to Spanish Flu, as did his daughter Marija, after which his wife died from grief. Marija had been in an unhappy marriage with Ivo's business partner and fellow shipping magnate Božo Banac (1883–1945), and sought solace in a platonic friendship with Croatian sculptor Ivan Meštrović (1883–1962), who was eventually commissioned to design the mausoleum.

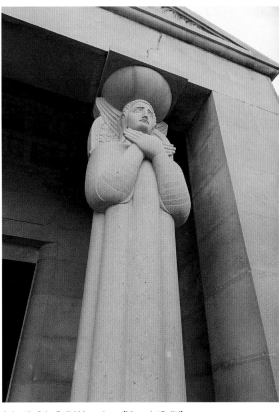

A detail of the Račić Mausoleum (Mauzolej Račić) overlooking Cavtat

Completed in 1922 in gleaming white Croatian limestone, the domed structure fused the latest Art Deco stylings with Christian and pagan motifs. Thus the neo-Classical portico is supported by striking angel-cum-priestess caryatids, and a frieze of winged sheep's' and rams' heads runs around the top. The bronze doors carry the signs of the zodiac, as well as depictions of the four Slavic apostles: Sava, Gregory, Cyril and Methodius. The latter pair invented Glagolitic, the oldest known Slavic alphabet, which is used for the door's inscriptions. Inside, the domed ceiling is carved with 136 angel faces, with four large angels ascending to heaven carrying dead infants (the four deceased family members).

48 A Renaissance Arboretum

Farther Afield (Trsteno), Trsteno Arboretum (note: buses depart for Trsteno every couple of hours from the Bus Station (Autobusni Kolodvor) at Gruž)

Twelve miles north-west of Dubrovnik's Old Town there is something special for Mediterranean garden lovers. The Trsteno Arboretum occupies a steep hillside sloping down to the Adriatic. Watered by a spring, this delightful pocket of greenery is one of Europe's oldest gardens.

The arboretum contains the summer villa of the noble Gučetić (Gozze) family, whose lineage can be traced back to the 10th-century (alternative Italian surnames, including Gozze, were used by the Ragusan nobility). According to legend a family member on his way to the Crusades inaugurated the arboretum with a single oak. In reality, it was created along with the villa in 1494 by Ivan Marinov Gučetić.

The arboretum is laid out across 450 manmade terraces rising almost 330 feet above sea level. The name 'Trsteno' comes from the Croatian *trstika* meaning 'reed', a reflection of the fact that the tall *Arundo donax* reed once grew here. The founding concepts of the original Renaissance arboretum still hold today, namely that architecture and nature be fused to create a harmonious whole, and that plants be as useful as they are decorous. These tenets are reflected in the geometrical ground plan of the garden, with its main axis leading down to a red-tiled pavilion overlooking the sea, and a citrus garden and olive press.

The original Renaissance-era villa was rebuilt following the great earthquake of 1667. The arboretum's most striking feature, the Fountain of Neptune, was reworked a century later in Baroque style, along with a chapel dedicated to St. Jerome. The fountain, which contains a statue of the Roman god Neptune, is fed by a fourteen-arch aqueduct to the rear.

During the Renaissance period, the distinguished philosopher and seven-time Rector of Ragusa, Nikola Gučetić (1549–1610), met with members of the Republic's Great Council at Trsteno (in those days they arrived not by road but by boat at the pretty little harbour below). They gathered around a stone garden table to discuss affairs of state, their pronouncements recorded by a scribe at a stone desk facing the opposite direction to preserve members' anonymity. Both table and desk survive in what is now called the Green Loggia.

Gučetić also gathered people of culture around him, including the poets Torquato Tasso (1544–1595) and Cvijeta Zuzorić (1552–1648), and the Venetian artist Titian (c. 1488/90–1576), whose studio painted the altarpiece in the Chapel of St. Michael on the hillside north of the village.

Each subsequent generation added to the arboretum. During the late 19th-century, for example, the western part of the arboretum was incorporated. Known as *Drvarica* (meaning 'wood'), it comprises a forested hillside tumbling down to a pathway at the water's edge.

Another personality at Trsteno was French nobleman Auguste de Marmont (1774–1852). He occupied the villa between 1806 and 1808, when Napoleon made him Duc de Raguse. Thereafter the arboretum reverted back to the Gučetić family, remaining in their hands until 1948, when

The Fountain of Neptune at the Trsteno Arboretum

it was acquired by the state. Now administered by the Croatian Academy of Sciences and Arts, the arboretum boasts over 450 cultivated species both indigenous and imported. These include trees such as Oriental Hornbeam, Mediterranean cypress, Aleppo pine, Sago Palm, and frothy pink Cape Myrtle, as well as other plants such as spiked agaves, black bamboo, Banksian roses and bougainvillea draped over the villa. There is also an historic olive grove, with fifteen old varieties.

Although the arboretum was damaged during the Croatian War (1991–1992), it has since been restored. Fortunately the magnificent pair of plane trees that have guarded the entrance for the last 500 years escaped unharmed.

49   Saltworks and Oysters Beds

Farther Afield (Veliki Ston), the Ston Saltworks (Solana Ston)
at Pelješki put 1 (note: Ston can be reached from Dubrovnik
by car, taxi or bus from the Bus Station (Autobusni Kolodvor)
at Gruž)

It came as a surprise to this author to learn that thirty miles north-west of Dubrovnik there are fortifications as impressive as those of Old Town. The villages of Veliki and Mali Ston (Great and Little Ston) together once constituted the second largest town in the Ragusan Republic. The 14th-century ramparts that encircle them stretch for over four miles and are today considered among the world's longest pre-modern fortifications.

That the walls sit either side of the neck of the Pelješac Peninsula explains the strategic importance of the location but there was another reason for their construction. Best seen from the walls overlooking Veliki Ston (Ston for short) are Europe's oldest saltworks. Still in operation today, they have an unbroken history stretching back over two thousand years.

With its deep water bay, low-lying coastal plain and close proximity to the mainland, Ston was made for salt production. The Romans, who arrived in 167 BC, were the first to exploit this valuable commodity. By the second half of the 14th-century, Ston had passed from the Bosnian principality of Hum to the Republic of Ragusa. Salt eventually provided the Republic with a third of its income, which explains the walls raised to protect production and the provisions made for handling salt in the Ragusan State Statute. It also accounts for the construction of Mali Ston as a port from where the salt was shipped to Ragusa and beyond, including the tables of the Habsburg Court in Vienna.

Salt production at Ston continues today much as it did during medieval times. Between April and October, sea water is let into a series of large shallow pools (or pans), where sun and wind begin the process of evaporation. As the water becomes more salty, it is channelled through sluices into the first of five parallel rows of smaller square pools. The water remains in each row for about a month depending on the weather before being moved onto the next. By the time it reaches the final row adjacent to the shoreline, the water is almost entirely evaporated and the salt nearly ready for harvesting. Harvesting has always been done by hand, originally by Ston's inhabitants but these days by students and seasonal workers. The only nod to modernity

Reflections in the historic saltpans at Ston

is the construction of a railway to move the salt to the warehouse in waggons rather than manually in sacks. In this way the Ston saltworks produce around 1500 tons of high quality salt annually. Guided tours of the saltworks are available by appointment (www.solanaston.hr).

For the epicurean explorer, there is another interesting industry to be discovered at Mali Ston, which can be reached by walking for half an hour along the top of the fortifications. From the waterfront, one can make out a grid of floating buoys. Suspended from these are ropes and nets on which oysters are cultivated. The earliest written documents on oyster collection at Mali Ston date from the 16th-century, with the first mention of deliberate oyster breeding a century later. At a London food fair in 1939, Mali Ston oysters were voted the world's finest. Many connoisseurs this still to be true because the European oyster *(Ostrea Edulis)* is raised in a unique mix of unpolluted sea water and mineral-laden fresh water from the Neretva River. Guided tours of the oyster beds followed by a tasting with accompanying local wines are recommended (www.malistonoysters.com).

Other locations nearby: 50

50 The Pelješac Wine Trail

Farther Afield (Pelješac), the vineyards of the Pelješac Peninsula, including the Miloš Winery at Boljenovići 15 near Ston (note: Ston and the Pelješac Peninsula can be reached from Dubrovnik by bus, car or taxi)

Croatia ranks well down the list of European wine-producing countries. Its annual output is currently one sixth that of neighbouring Serbia's yearly production, and a mere one percent of Italy's yield. This doesn't mean, however, that Croatian wines should be dismissed, indeed far from it. Croatian wine has a venerable history stretching back into antiquity, with some of its finest bottles produced on the sun-soaked Pelješac Peninsula, north-west of Dubrovnik.

The wild Pelješac Peninsula is one of over 300 geographically-defined wine-producing areas in Croatia. Specifically it lies within the Central and South Dalmatia sub-region, which encompasses the coastline from Istria in the north down to the southern tip of the country. Limestone is the key to successful vinification here. It shapes much of the Dinaric Alps, which form a border between the coast and the hinterland. As it erodes, so it creates a rocky landscape known as *karst*. Sandy free-draining soils gather in hollows in the *karst* and it is here that

Plavac Mali ('little blue') graped in the vineyards of the Pelješac Peninsula

vines flourish, especially on the peninsula's south-facing slopes. Local vintners say that the sun ripens their vines from three directions: directly from the sun, mirrored off the sea, and reflected off the white *karst* itself.

Vineyards cover large tracts of the Pelješac Peninsula's southern coast starting around Ston and stretching north-west as far as the outskirts of the town of Orebić near the peninsula's tip. The dominant grape variety is the indigenous *Plavac Mali* ('little blue') which produces fruity, full-bodied red wine, with lots of tannins and high alcohol content (13–15%). The harsh arid conditions and sea breezes result in low yields but distinctive flavours.

Wine buffs can travel the length of the peninsula, stopping in at wineries along the way. Some larger concerns, such as the Peninsula Wine Bar & Shop at Donja Banda centar 2 and Saints Hills at Zagruda bb, operate their own visitors' centres (note that addresses appended with 'bb' *(bez broja)* mean there is no street number). Others remain family concerns that sell their produce from home and seasonal roadside stalls, notably in the coastal Dingač area just east of Orebić. Here the villages of Potomje and Postup produce excellent reds that even boast their own appellation. Harvesting the grapes is punishing work though, with pickers obliged to abseil down some of the steepest slopes!

For those visiting the salt pans at Ston, it is only a short journey out to the Miloš Winery at Boljenovići 15 (see no. 49). The founder, Frano Miloš, bought up what was formerly a state winery after the fall of Communism and became one of the first of the Pelješac vintners to carve out an international reputation. The terraced vineyards here illustrate perfectly how the peninsula's *karst* scenery has been adapted to accommodate the production of grapes. It is recommended to book a visit in advance (www.milos.hr).

There are several other worthwhile sights on the Pelješac Peninsula. These include the town of Orebič, with its old sea captains' houses, small maritime museum and 15th-century hillside Monastery of Our Lady of Angels (Franjevački samostan Gospe od Anđela), with votives donated by grateful seafarers. There is also the impressive Pelješac Bridge (Pelješki most) opened in 2022. It spans the sea channel between the Pelješac Peninsula and Komarna on the mainland providing a much-needed fixed link between Croatia's south-eastern exclave (including Dubrovnik) and the rest of the country, bypassing Bosnia and Herzegovina's short coastal strip at Neum. Designed by Slovenian engineer Marjan Pipenbaher (b. 1957), the bridge is a multi-span cable-stayed construction with a total length of 7,887 feet.

Other locations nearby: 49

51 The Mljet National Park

The Islands (Mljet), the Mljet National Park (Nacionalni park Mljet) (note: ferries depart from the port at Gruž to Mljet's port of Sobra, as does the fast catamaran during the tourist season, which then continues on to Polače and returns from Pomena)

Mljet is the largest island in the Dubrovnik Archipelago. Known for its legendary history and natural beauty, it is easily reached either by boat from Gruž to the island's port of Sobra, or else by fast catamaran (during the tourist season) to Polače, a village on the edge of the Mljet National Park (Nacionalni park Mljet).

It has been claimed locally that Mljet is the mythical island of Ogygia. Mentioned in Book Five of Homer's *Odyssey*, it was on Ogygia that King Odysseus was shipwrecked during his return home from the Trojan War, and held captive for seven years by the nymph Calypso. Despite her offer of immortality in return for marriage, Odysseus' thoughts were only for his wife, Penelope, and he was eventually freed by direct order of Zeus. Homer's description of Ogygia certainly matches Mljet, including a vine-draped cave like that occupied by Calypso, and place names that include the word *baba* ('old lady'), which could confirm the belief that Calypso remained on Ogygia well into old age. There is no hard evidence though and it is just as likely that Ogygia was the island of Gozo, as claimed by the Maltese, or the Greek island of Othonoi, or even the utopian land of Atlantis.

Mljet is also linked to another ancient tale, namely that of Saint Paul (c. 5–c. 65 AD). Tradition states that his famous shipwreck whilst on the way from Jerusalem to Rome occurred on the island. Again real proof is lacking and once more a parallel claim is made for Malta. What is definite is that like Dubrovnik, Mljet was originally occupied by Illyrians and Romans, and later came under the sway of Byzantium.

The most forested of Croatia's islands, and one of the most beautiful, Mljet is best known for its national park, which occupies the western part of the island. Accessed by mini bus, taxi or bicycle (cars are not allowed), the park is criss-crossed with signposted walking trails. Don't miss the tidal Great and Small Lakes (Veliko and Malo Jezero), which join the sea by means of the Soline Channel. In the Great Lake there is an island – so an island on an island – on which stands the 12th-century Benedictine Monastery and Church of St Mary (Crkva sv. Marija). Accessible by public boat, the monastery complex has Romanesque, Renaissance and Baroque features, as well as a fortified

Canoeists enjoy Great Lake (Veliko Jezero) in the Mljet National Park (Nacionalni park Mljet)

tower built as protection against pirates. Closed by Napoleon in 1808, it subsequently became a hotel and is now in the hands of the Catholic Diocese of Dubrovnik.

The lakes are surrounded by ancient pine forests beneath which grow tiny pink cyclamen. If you're at the coast you might be lucky enough to catch a glimpse of the rare Mediterranean monk seal *(Monachus monachus)*. The Mljet National Park is after all the oldest protected marine area in the Mediterranean, founded in 1960.

Mljet is a paradise for those who enjoy sea swimming, with several scenic coves at Pomena, Polače and Saplunara. Pomena is also home to the island's only hotel, the aptly-named Odysseus, and is a staging post on the annual 3-day South Dalmatian Sailing Regatta between Orebić on the Pelješac Peninsula and Dubrovnik. Polače boasts a Roman waterfront palace so large that the road runs right through it!

Traditions die hard on Mljet. Local products still made the old fashioned way include woven baskets known as *Mljetska Kosice* and conical fishing traps called *Mljetska Vrsa*. There is distinctive island embroidery, too, done mainly with red, green and yellow threads.

52 Escape to the Elaphites

The Islands (Elaphiti Islands), a visit to the islands of Koločep, Lopud and Šipan (note: a foot-ferry departs from the port at Gruž twice times a day as does a car ferry once or twice a day)

When Dubrovnik gets too much, one can always escape to the Elaphiti Islands (Elafitski otoci). This thirteen-island archipelago may lie just offshore from Dubrovnik but it represents another world. Sparsely populated with a welcome lack of motor vehicles, they are the domain of sleepy farms, wild nature, ancient churches and abandoned palaces, where time passes slowly and little has changed in a long time.

The Elaphites (Elafiti) are part of what geographers call a 'Dalmatian Coastline', that is a series of peaks and troughs running parallel to the coast formed by the movement of the earth's tectonic plates. Sea level rise in postglacial times left only the peaks visible in the form of narrow chains of offshore islands (see no. 43).

The Elaphites comprise eight such islands (Daksa, Jakljan, Koločep, Lopud, Olipa, Ruda, Šipan and Tajan), as well as five islets (Crkvine, Goleč, Kosmeč, Mišnjak and Sveti Andrija). Of these, the three main islands are Šipan, Lopud, Koločep, which between them are home to barely a thousand people. Connected by a daily foot-ferry from Dubrovnik's port at Gruž, they make for a good round-trip, with plenty of interest along the way.

The island closest to Dubrovnik and the smallest of the three is Koločep, just three miles away. Important for shipbuilding and coral diving during Ragusan times, it has two villages, Gornje Čelo on the south-east side and Donje Čelo on the north-west (where the ferry calls). They are connected by a delightful walled path that runs through orchards and olive groves. Side tracks radiate out through pine forests to isolated coves and no less than seven medieval churches.

Next in size comes Lopud. Known by the Romans as *Insula Media* because of its midway position between Koločep and Šipan, it is today the most populated and developed of the islands. The homonymous village illustrates the island's rich history, with its elegant harbour promenade lined with stone houses, lorded over by an abandoned 15th-century Franciscan monastery and a ruined Gothic-Renaissance rector's palace. Also on the promenade is the 19th-century Đorđić-Mayneri pleasure garden, a chapel endowed by famous native shipowner Miho Pracat (1522–1607), and the abandoned 1930s-era Grand Hotel designed by architect Nikola Dobrović (1897–1967), the Father of Adriatic Modernism.

Šipan is the largest and most fertile of the islands, and the one farthest from Dubrovnik. It has two major villages, Suđurađ in the south and Šipanska Luka in the north, both of which are visited by the ferry. Šipan was largely tamed during the time of the Ragusan Republic by aristocrats, merchants and sea captains. This is most evident in the great cultivated valley that stretches between the villages, dotted with vineyards, orchards and olive groves (remarkably Šipan holds the world record for having the most olive trees per capita). It accounts for why Šipan was once the richest of the Elaphites, a fact reflected in the island's thirty-four churches and the ruined summer residences that line the valley, notably that of humanist, poet and archbishop, Lodovico Bec-

Communing with nature on the peaceful Elaphiti island of Šipan

cadelli (1501–1572). Suđurađ's built legacy includes a pair of 16th-century summer palaces commissioned by the Skočibuha family of merchants, and the unmissable fortified Church of the Holy Ghost (Crkva sv. Duh) on the hill above (see no. 16).

The adventurous may wish to stray from the island's main thoroughfare and strike up towards the jagged escarpment that defines the island's west coast. Covered in trees and scrub, it is home to wild boar, with sea cliffs that beetle away to the sea below. You have been warned…

53 The Daksa Massacre

The Islands (Daksa), Daksa Island (Otočić Daksa) at the mouth of the Rijeka Dubrovačka (note: access to the island is by private launch only)

At the mouth of the Rijeka Dubrovačka, north of Dubrovnik, is Daksa Island (Otočić Daksa). Ferries sailing between the port at Gruž and the Elaphiti Islands (Elafitski otoci) pass by daily but none stop. For not only is Daksa uninhabited but it also has a dark history.

Pine-covered Daksa is tiny, the smallest of the Elaphites. Things started peacefully enough for it in 1281, when a local nobleman, one Sabo Getaldić, founded a monastery and church. A decade later, by the terms of his will, the property passed to the Franciscans and for the next few centuries Daksa was a haven of peace. So much so that Ragusa's celebrated poet Ivan Gundulić (1589–1638) came to the island to pen his *Suze sina razmetnoga* (Tears of the Prodigal Son) in which he presents the three basics of Christianity: sin, repentance and redemption. Peace was only broken in 1808, when the monastery was forcibly evacuated for strategic reasons by the French and fortifications erected.

Worse was to follow during the Second World War. Efforts to keep Yugoslavia out of the conflict had been dashed in 1940 with Italy's entry into the war on the side of the Axis powers. Yugoslavia was now encircled by hostile forces and partitioned to create a separate state of Croatia, including Dubrovnik. It was only in name though and in 1941 Italian forces entered Dubrovnik and held it until Italy's capitulation in 1943. Thereafter the city fell to Nazi Germany, albeit with staunch resistance from the Communist-led Yugoslav Partisans led by Jozip Broz Tito (1892–1980). It was their 8th Dalmatian Corps that eventually liberated Dubrovnik on 18th October 1944.

Liberation came at a price though as Partisan units hunted down anyone suspected of being either a Nazi collaborator or an anti-Communist. In Dubrovnik over 300 men were arrested, including not only politicians, intellectuals and business people but also farmers, a tax officer and a school janitor. Most were innocent but the Partisans wanted blood.

On the night of 24th October, several dozen prisoners were shipped over to Daksa Island. There they were marched up into the trees, stripped, forced to dig their own graves, and then shot from behind. First to die were three monks from the order that had pro-

Dusk falls on Daksa Island and bad memories are rekindled

vided peace on Daksa for so many centuries. Other victims included the Jesuit priest Petar Perica (1881–1944), who composed the famous Croatian song *Rajska Djevo, Kraljice Hrvata* (Celestial Virgin, Queen of the Croats), and Niko Koprivica, the mayor of Dubrovnik. A few days' later bills were posted around Dubrovnik announcing that 36 people had been found guilty of treason and executed. No evidence was ever presented though and no-one ever tried for the deaths.

The executions left the citizens of Dubrovnik shaken. They were warned against visiting Daksa to look for human remains and public discussion was forbidden. Right up until independence in the early 1990s, the island remained off-limits. Little wonder that various horror stories were whispered in the shadows, including how the lighthouse keeper's children saw human hands emerging from the soil.

Only in 2009 were the bones of fifty three people exhumed from two mass graves and re-interred. Today the victims are remembered by several of headstones erected at the execution site in the south of the island. Those who care to pay their respects will also find the ruined monastery with its Church of Our Lady, and the now automated lighthouse erected by the Austrians in 1873 (see no. 54).

54 Living in a Lighthouse

The Islands (Lapad), the Grebeni Lighthouse (Svjetionik Grebeni) off the Lapad Peninsula (note: the island is only accessible by private launch and only for those staying in the lighthouse)

When it comes to dream accommodation in Croatia, many visitors book a room with a sea view. In most cases of course they will be sharing their idyll with other like-minded holidaymakers. For those craving an exclusive outlook, however, and a 360 degree one at that, the Croatian coastline has the answer. Why not book a holiday in a lighthouse?

For a century and a half, a string of almost 50 lighthouses has guided mariners off the rocks and reefs of the Dalmatian coast. This stretch of coast is a particularly dangerous one. It was formed when sea levels rose following the last ice age, drowning the low-lying areas of the Dinaric Alps, which plunge down to the coast here. This converted valleys into sounds and hill tops into dangerous offshore archipelagos.

It was during Dubrovnik's time as part of the Kingdom of Dalmatia that the Austrians built most of the lighthouses. Initially they were manned by lighthouse keepers, who lived on-site with their families. Those days are gone now and the lights that are still used are automatic. As a result, several of these idiosyncratic structures have been acquired by entrepreneurial property developers and their domestic quarters converted for use as unusual holiday homes.

A fine example is the lighthouse at the western extremity of the Grebeni archipelago, a chain of otherwise uninhabited islets off the coast of Dubrovnik's Lapad Peninsula (not surprisingly the name 'Lapad' is derived from the Latin word for rock). Built by the Austrians in 1872 to guide shipping into the port at Gruž, the sturdy, single-storey Grebeni Lighthouse (Svjetionik Grebeni) is square in plan, its lantern perched high on a red-tiled roof. Like the lighthouse keepers of old, todays guests are conveyed the third of a mile from the shore by private launch. The pilot then returns to shore but remains at guests' disposal by telephone in case of an emergency.

After disembarkation, guests climb a zig-zag flight of rock-cut steps to reach the lighthouse. Stylishly converted in 2012 to suit modern tastes, it consists of three bedrooms, two bathrooms, a kitchen and a living room, with electricity provided by solar panels. The views from the windows are stupendous, whether looking out across the Adriatic

The Grebeni Lighthouse (Svjetionik Grebeni) provides unusual holiday accommodation

at sunset or else back to land and the city lights. Outside the lighthouse there is a stone terrace with a small seawater swimming pool although most guests will probably be tempted to dip their toes in the sea proper. Those who enjoy underwater exploration will be pleased to hear that not far from Grebeni rests the wreck of the steamer *Toranto*. It sank in 1943 with its Dubrovnik-bound cargo of flour and tractors after hitting a floating mine.

As night falls, guests not easily scared might like to reflect on a story from 1958. During a terrific storm a huge rock was allegedly hurled by waves through one of the lighthouse windows. So shocked was the keeper and his family that they left Grebeni the next day and never returned. Grebeni Lighthouse can be booked at www.luva-villas.com.

Dubrovnik's Elaphiti Islands (Elafitski otoci) boast three more Austrian-built lighthouses, all on uninhabited islets, although none can currently be rented. One on Sveti Andrija marks a reef south of Lopud, an island once popular with coral divers; a second on Olipa protects ships passing south of the Pelješac Peninsula; and a third on Daksa guides shipping outside Dubrovnik's deep-water port at Gruž (see no. 53).

55 The Curse of Lokrum Island

The Islands (Lokrum), Lokrum Island south of Old Town (note: a daily ferry service departs every half hour for Lokrum from the Old Port (Stara Luka) during the summer months)

Lokrum Island sits a third of a mile south of Dubrovnik's Old Town. For a thousand years its fortunes have waxed and waned, giving rise to several colourful legends and even talk of a curse. The truth, however, is rather less romantic.

Local lore claims that in 1192 the English King Richard the Lionheart (1157–1199) was shipwrecked on Lokrum on his return from the Crusades, and in exchange for shelter vowed to build a church (see no. 11). In actual fact a Benedictine monastery and church was founded on the island in 1023 in gratitude for a fire in Dubrovnik's Old Town being successfully extinguished. The island's name, which comes from the Latin *acrumen* meaning 'sour tasting', recalls the citrus trees cultivated by the monks.

The origin of the curse dates from 1798, when the Ragusan Senate sold the Lokrum, and the monastery was closed by papal decree. Before departing, the monks allegedly left a trail of candle wax around their monastery's perimeter, cursing any future newcomers that might cross it. Believers in the efficacy of the curse cite two events that occurred in 1859. First, the Austrian ship *Triton* exploded off Lokrum killing most of her crew. Secondly, when Austrian Archduke Ferdinand Maximilian (1832–1867) arrived to honour the dead he fell in love with the island and purchased it, incorporating the abandoned monastery into a flamboyant summer palace. In 1863 he accepted the title Emperor of Mexico from Napoleon III (1808–1873) but was executed by Mexican Republican forces. Far from being the curse, however, Maximilian's death was no surprise since the French had used him as an unwitting proxy to exact revenge on Mexico for an unpaid debt. As for the *Triton*, its demise was recorded as misadventure.

After Maximilian's death Lokrum was surrendered to the Habsburgs. When Crown Prince Rudolf (1858–1889) arrived to spend part of his honeymoon on the island, earth tremors are said to have been heard. Seismic activity, however, is relatively common in the area, including a great earthquake in 1667 that damaged the monastery church. Then in 1889 Rudolf died in a suicide pact with his mistress in a hunting lodge outside Vienna. Had the curse struck again? It seems more likely that the prince saw no escape from his stagnant marriage and dreaded the prospect of becoming emperor.

After the First World War, Lokrum became part of the new Kingdom of Yugoslavia and the curse goes to ground. Not until the Croatian War of the early 1990s did the island again attract bad luck when it was hit by Serbian rockets. This was no curse either though since many more missiles rained down on Dubrovnik's Old Town.

One final episode attributed to the curse came in 2014, when the European Rabbit (Oryctolagus cuniculus) reached the island and caused considerable damage to the Botanical Garden established in 1959. Once more though there was a curse-free explanation to hand, namely that Lokrum despite being a Special Reserve had been for a while left unguarded.

Austrian and Mexican emblems adorn a window of Archduke Maximilian's palace on Lokrum

So visitors to Lokrum can safely ignore the curse and instead enjoy the island's pleasures. These include not only the Botanical Garden, with its collection of Eucalyptus trees (the largest outside Australia), and the ruined monastery-cum-palace but also the French Fort Royal (1806) on the island's highest point, a salt lake dubbed the Dead Sea (Mrtvo More), a ruined 16th-century quarantine facility *(Lazaretto)*, and the many peacocks introduced from the Canary Isles by the doomed Maximilian.

Opening Times

Correct at time of going to press but may be subject to change.

Boninovo Cemetery (Groblje Boninovo), Boninovo, Ulica Između tri Crkve 1, daily 7am–8pm

Cable Car (Uspinjača), Ploče, Ulica Kralja Petra Krešimira IV. 10A, Apr & Oct 9am–9pm, May 9am–11pm, Jun–Sep 9am–12am

Caffe Bar Libertina, Old Town, Zlatarska ulica 3, daily 10am–2pm

Cathedral of the Assumption (Katedrala Velike Gospe), Old Town, Ulica kneza Damjana Jude 1, Mon–Sat 8am–7pm, Sun 11am–7pm; Treasury Mon–Sat 8am–4pm, Sun 11am–5pm

Church of Sigurata (Crkva Sigurata), Old Town, Ulica od Sigurate 13, daily 9am–5pm

Church of St. Blaise (Crkva sv. Blaža), Old Town, Luža Ulica, Mon–Sat 9am–12pm, 4–6pm, Sun 7am–1pm (Aug 7am–12am)

Church of St. Ignatius (Crkva sv. Ignacija), Old Town, Poljana Ruđera Boškovića, daily 6.30am–10pm; English-language Mass Jun–Sep Sun 11am

Church of Sigurata (Crkva Sigurata), Old Town, Ulica od Sigurate 13, daily 9am–5pm

Church of St. Stephen (Crkva sv. Stjepana), Old Town, Ulica Stulina, the ruins are visible all hours

Convent of St. Clare (Samostan Sveta Klare), Old Town, Poljana Paska Miličevića, daily 10am–10.30pm

Croata Museum Concept Store, Old Town, Ulica Pred Dvorom 2, Mon–Sat 10am–8pm

Dominican Monastery and Museum (Dominikanski samostan i muzej), Old Town, Ulica svetog Dominika 4, daily 9am–6pm

Dubrovnik Beer Company, Gruž, Obala pape Ivana Pavla II 15, Tap Room daily 11am–12am, guided tours 5pm by appointment only at www.dubrovackapivovara.hr

Dubrovnik City Walls (Dubrovačke gradske zidine), Old Town, Pile Gate (Vrata od Pila), daily 8am–7pm

Dubrovnik Mosque (Masjid Dubrovnik), Old Town, Ulica Miha Pracata 3, daily 10am–1pm

Dubrovnik Natural History Museum (Prirodoslovni muzej Dubrovnik), Old Town, Ulica Androvićeva 1, Mon–Sat 10am–6pm

Dubrovnik Synagogue (Dubrovačka sinagoga), Old Town, Žudioska ulica 5, daily 9am–8pm

Fort Lovrijenac (Tvrđava Lovrijenac), Pile, Ulica Skalini dr. Marka Foteza, daily 8am–4pm

Fort Minčeta (Tvrđava Minčeta), Old Town, Ulica Ispod Minčete 9, daily 8am–7.30pm

Fort Revelin (Tvrđava Revelin), Old Town, daily 8am–4am; Archaeological Exhibitions (Arheološke izložbe) Thu–Tue 9am–6pm

Franciscan Monastery (Franjevaški samostan), Old Town, Poljana Paska Miličevića 4, daily 9am–6pm

Gradac Park, Pile, Ulica don Frana Bulića, open 24 hours

Grebeni Lighthouse (Svjetionik Grebeni), Lapad, accommodation can be booked at www.luva-villas.com

Gruž Market, Gruž, Obala Stjepana Radića 21, Mon–Sat 7am–12pm

House of Marin Držić (Marin Držić's hus), Old Town, Ulica Široka 7, Tue–Sun 9am–8.30pm

Konoba Dundo Maroje, Old Town, Kovačka ulica 1, daily 11am–2am

Lazareti Quarantine Infirmaries, Ploče, Ulica Frana Supila 8–10, courtyards open daily 9am–6pm

Marin Držić Theatre (Kazalište Marina Držića), Old Town, Ulica Pred Dvorom, for current productions visit www.kmd.hr

Maritime Museum (Pomorski muzej), Old Town, Fort St. John (Tvrđava sv. Ivana), Thu–Tue 9am–6pm

Miloš Winery, Pelješac, Boljenovići 15, daily 10am–6pm

Mljet National Park (Nacionalni park Mljet), Mljet, daily 8am–8pm

Morning Market, Old Town, Gundulićeva poljana, Mon–Fri until 1pm, Sat all day

Museum of Modern Art Dubrovnik (Umjetnikča Galerija Dubrovnik) (MoMAD), Ploče, Ulica Frana Supila 23, Tue–Sun 9am–8pm

Orsula Park (Park Orsula), Ploče, Ulica Frana Sulipa, open all hours

Račić Mausoleum (Mauzolej Račić), Cavtat, Cemetery of St. Roch, cemetery open all hours

Rector's Palace (Knežev dvor), Old Town, Ulica Pred Dvorom 3, Thu–Tue 9am–6pm

Red History Museum (Muzej crvene povijesti), Gruž, Svetog križa 3, daily 12pm–6pm (final admission 5pm)

Rupe Ethnographic Museum (Ethnografic Museum Rupe), Old Town, Ulica Od Rupa 3, Thu–Tue 9am–6pm

Serbian Orthodox Church of the Holy Annunciation (Srpske pravoslavne crkve Svetog blagoveštenja), Old Town, Ulica od Puča 8, daily 8am–9pm

Sorkočević Palace, Old Town, Poljana Marina Držića 3, Mon–Sat 10am–7pm

Sponza Palace (Palača Sponza), Old Town, Stradun 2, daily 8am–7pm; Dubrovnik State Archives (Državni arhiv u Dubrovniku) Reading Room by appointment only Mon– Fri 8.15am–3pm, Sat 8.15am–1pm

Ston Saltworks (Solana Ston), Veliki Ston, Pelješki put 1, Apr–Jun 8am–6pm, Jul–Sep 7am–7pm, Oct–Mar 7am–2pm, guided tours by appointment at www.solanaston.hr

Trsteno Arboretum, Trsteno, daily 7am–7pm

War Photo Limited, Old Town, Antuninska ulica 6, Apr & Oct daily 10am–5pm (last admission 4pm), May–Sep 10am–10pm (last admission 9pm)

A classic Old Town view looking down Ulica Naljeskoviceva (see no. 1)

Further Reading

GUIDEBOOKS & MAPS
Insight Guides Flexi Map Dubrovnik (APA Publications), Insight Guides, 2017

Visible Cities: Dubrovnik (Annabel Barber), Somerset, 2006

DK Top Ten Dubrovnik and the Dalmatian Coast (DK Eyewitness), DK Eyewitness Travel, 2022

Lonely Planet Pocket Dubrovnik and the Dalmatian Coast (Peter Dragicevich), Lonely Planet Publications, 2022

Rick Steves Snapshot Dubrovnik (Cameron Hewitt & Rick Steves), Rick Steves, 2020

Explore Dubrovnik Insight Guide (Insight Guides), APA Publications, 2018

Marco Polo Dubrovnik and the Dalmatian Coast (Marco Polo), Mairdumont, 2019

Lokrum (Antun Ničetić), Dubrovnik, 2009

Rough Guide to Dubrovnik (Rough Guides), Rough Guides, 2019

Dalmatia (Eric Whelpton), Robert Hale, 1954

HISTORY
Expelling the Plague: the Health Office and the implementation of quarantine in Dubrovnik, 1377–1533 (Zlata Blažina-Tomić & Vesna Blažina), McGill-Queen's University Press, 2015

Dubrovnik (Ragusa): A Classic City-state (Francis W. Carter), Seminar Press, 1972

The Republic of Dubrovnik Final Crisis (Vesna Čučić), CroLIbertas, 2017

Dubrovnik in War (Miljenko Foretić & Vlado Gotovac), Matica hrvatska, 2000

Dubrovnik: A History (Robin Harris), Saqi Books, 2006

Dubrovnik Between History & Legend (Marko Margaritoni), Dubrovnik State Archives, 2001

The Jews of Dubrovnik (Vesna Miović), Foto Studio Placa, 2015

Wisdom at the Crossroads: True Stories from the time of the Republic of Dubrovnik Republic and the Ottoman Empire (Vesna Miović), Kartolina, 2011

Dubrovnik Revisited (Slobodan Prosperov Novak), Biblioteka Ambrozia, 2005

The Story of Dubrovnik (Slavica Stojan), Ogranak Matice hrvatske u Dubrovniku, 2021

Croatia: A Nation Forged in War (Marcus Tanner), Yale Nota Bene, 1997

The Nobility of Dubrovnik (Nenad Vekarić), Croatian Academy of Sciences and Arts, 2019

Between the Double Eagle and the Crescent (Zdenko Zlatar), Columbia University Press, 1992

Dubrovnik's Merchants and Capital in the Ottoman Empire 1520–1620, (Zdenko Zlatar), Isis Press, 2011

MUSEUMS & GALLERIES
Maritime Museum Guide (Ana Kaznačić & Ljerka Dunatov), Dubrovnik Museums, 2012

Friars Minor Pharmacy: 700 Years of Health in Dubrovnik (Stipe Nosić), Dubrovnik 2017

ART & ARCHITECTURE
Dubrovnik Cathedral (Ante Dračevac), Privredni Vjesnik, 1988

The Cathedral of the Assumption of the Virgin in Dubrovnik (Ed. Katarina Horvat-Levaj), City Parish of the Assumption, 2016

The Collegiate Church of St Blaise in Dubrovnik (Katarina Horvat-Levaj & Antun Baće), ArTresor, 2019

The Dominican Priory in Dubrovnik (Stjepan Krasić), Dominikanski Samostan Sv. Dominika, 2002

Walls and Gateways: Contested Heritage in Dubrovnik (Celine Motzfeldt Loades), Berghahn, 2022

Dubrovnik Renaissance Gardens : Genesis and Design Characteristics (Bruno Šišić), Croatian Academy of Sciences and Arts, 2008

ILLUSTRATED BOOKS
Dubrovnik (Fernando Espinosa Chauvin), Trama Diseno, 2009

Dubrovnik (Damir Fabijanić), Iće&piće, 2018

Dubrovnik and the Elaphites : Heart of the Adriatic Riviera (James Fforde & Christian Smith), Lowell, 2009

Dubrovnik (Cvito Fiskovic), Jugoslavija, 1964

Dubrovnik (Antun Traviska), Forum, 2005

TRAVEL WRITING
A Memory of Ragusa (Leonard Green), Holbrook, 1929

Croatia through Writers' Eyes (Ed. by Peter Frankopan, Francis Gooding & Stephen Lavington), Eland, 2006

TOUR COMPANIES
www.walkingtourdubrovnik.com (Walking tours based around storytelling)

www.dubrovnikgameofthronestour.com & www.kingslandingdubrovnik.com (Game of Thrones' Tours)

www.jewishdubrovnik.com (specialist-led Jewish history tour)

WEBSITES
www.tzdubrovnik.hr (Dubrovnik Tourist Board)

www.visitdubrovnik.hr (Dubrovnik and Neretva County Tourist Board)

www.thedubrovniktimes.com (Local news and culture updates)

www.lostindubrovnik.com (Cultural, dining and other recommendations)

www.inyourpocket.com/dubrovnik (Extensive cultural and leisure listings)

Acknowledgements

For kind permission to take photographs, as well as for arranging access and the provision of information, the following people are most gratefully acknowledged:

Nikoleta Belemečić (Dubrovačka baština), Dragana Bratić (Dubrovnik Synagogue), Kevin, Julia & Hazel Lily Brooks, Božo Burić (Dubrovnik Tourist Board/Turistička zajednica grada Dubrovnika), Luciano 'Lući'Capurso (Café-Bar Libertina), Rainer Dornbusch (Lokrum Island), Žarko Dragojević (Marin Držić Theatre), Maro Dubravčić (Hotel Grand Villa Argentina), Mili Dunđer (Konoba Dubrava), Xenia & Luka Kapor, Dubrovnik Mosque, Jordi Faus, Nenad Gorjanović (LUVA Villas), Igor Hajdarhodžić (Art Studio Igor Hajdarhodžić), Vanessa Kamić, Oliver Lehmann, Mateo Kalinić (Gornji Ugao Tower), Ana Micus (State Archives in Dubrovnik), Museums of Dubrovnik (Muzeji I Galerije Grada Dubrovnika), BožoPetric&RadePleša (Miho Pracat Seamens' Club), Magdalena Prkut (Museum of Modern Art Dubrovnik), Đurđica Sambrailo (Croata Museum Concept Store), Dario Ševelj & Tereza Čabrilo (Dubrovnik Beer Company), Dubravka Tullio, Jadranka Sulić Šprem & Josip Čorak (Natural History Museum), Đivo Vidjević (Cathedral of the Assumption), and Celine Wawruschka.

Special thanks go to Ekke Wolf (www.typic.at) for creating the layout, Wade Goddard (War Photo Limited) for good conversation and help when my camera broke, Đurđica Sambrailo for her photos of Caffe Bar Libertina, and Violeta Vukanovic for the accommodation.

Thanks also to my mother Mary and great cousin James Dickinson for bringing interesting news items to my attention, Dubravka Grujić for punctuation and pronunciation, Simon Laffoley for his expertise with picture selection and photo editing, and Digital Bits for managing my website.

Finally, heartfelt thanks to Roswitha Reisinger for her tireless support of my work and wonderful company on field trips, and to my late father Trevor for inspiring me to track down things unique, hidden and unusual in the first place.

Imprint

1st Edition published by The Urban Explorer, 2023
A division of Duncan J. D. Smith
contact@duncanjdsmith.com
www.onlyinguides.com
www.duncanjdsmith.com

Graphic design: Stefan Fuhrer
Typesetting, picture editing and cover design: Ekke Wolf
Maps: www.netmaps.net & www.scalablemaps.com
Printed and bound in Dubai by Oriental Press

The rose window of the Church of St. Saviour (Crkva sv. Spasa) (see no. 6)

ISBN 978-3-9504218-8-0

MIX
Paper | Supporting responsible forestry
FSC
www.fsc.org
FSC® C004800